40-Day Journey with Madeleine L'Engle

Other books in the

40-DAY *Journey*

Series

40-Day Journey with Joan Chittister
Beverly Lanzetta, Editor

40-Day Journey with Dietrich Bonhoeffer
Ron Klug, Editor

40-Day Journey with Martin Luther
Gracia M. Grindal, Editor

40-Day Journey with Kathleen Norris
Kathryn Haueisen, Editor

40-Day Journey with Parker J. Palmer
Henry F. French, Editor

40-DAY Journey

WITH MADELEINE L'ENGLE

40-Day Journey Series

Isabel Anders, Editor

Augsburg Books

Minneapolis

40-DAY JOURNEY WITH MADELEINE L'ENGLE

Cover art: Madeleine L'Engle, circa 1987. Used by permission of Crosswicks, Ltd.
Cover design: Christy Barker
Interior design: PerecType, Nashville, Tenn.

Library of Congress Cataloging-in-Publication Data

40-day journey with Madeleine L' Engle / Isabel Anders, editor.
    p. cm. — (The 40 day journey series)
Includes bibliographical references and index.
ISBN 978-0-8066-5762-2 (alk. paper)
1. Spiritual life—Christianity. 2. Devotional exercises. 3. L'Engle, Madeleine. I. Anders, Isabel, 1946–
II. Title: Forty day journey with Madeleine L' Engle.

BV4501.3.A14 2009
242—dc22

2008031808

The paper used in this publication meets the minimum requirements of American National Standard for Informa-
tion Sciences—Permanence of Paper for Printed Library Materials, ANSI Z329.48-1984.

Printed in Canada

12   11   10   09   08   1   2   3   4   5   6   7   8   9   10

CONTENTS

SERIES INTRODUCTION

Imagine spending forty days with a great spiritual guide who has both the wisdom and the experience to help you along the path of your own spiritual journey. Imagine being able to listen to and question spiritual guides from the past and the present. Imagine being, as it were, mentored by women and men who have made their own spiritual journey and have recorded the landmarks, detours, bumps in the road, potholes, and wayside rests that they encountered along the way—all to help others (like you) who must make their own journey.

The various volumes in Augsburg Books' *40-Day Journey Series* are all designed to do just that—to lead you to where your mind and heart and spirit long to go. As Augustine once wrote: *"You have made us for yourself, O Lord, and our heart is restless until it rests in you."* The wisdom you will find in the pages of this series of books will give you the spiritual tools and direction to find that rest. But there is nothing quietistic in the spirituality you will find here. Those who would guide you on this journey have learned that the heart that rests in God is one that lives with deeper awareness, deeper creativity, deeper energy, and deeper passion and commitment to the things that matter to God.

An ancient Chinese proverb states the obvious: the journey of a thousand miles begins with the first step. In a deep sense, books in the *40-Day Journey Series* are first steps on a journey that will not end when the 40 days are over. No one can take the first step (or any step) for you.

Imagine that you are on the banks of the Colorado River. You are here to go white-water rafting for the first time and your guide has just described the experience, telling you with graphic detail what to expect. It sounds both exciting and frightening. You long for the experience but are somewhat disturbed, anxious, uncertain in the face of the danger that promises to accompany you on the journey down the river. The guide gets into the raft. She will accompany you on the journey, *but she can't take the journey for you.* If you want to experience the wildness of the river, the raw beauty of the canyon, the camaraderie of adventurers, and the mystery of a certain oneness with nature (and nature's creator), then you've got to get in the boat.

This book in your hand is like that. It describes the journey, provides a "raft," and invites you to get in. Along with readings from your spiritual guide, you will find scripture to mediate on, questions to ponder, suggestions for personal journaling, guidance in prayer, and a prayer for the day. If done faithfully each day, you will find the wisdom and encouragement you need to integrate meaningful spiritual practices into your daily life. And when the 40-day journey is over, it will no longer be the guide's description of the journey that stirs your longing for God, but *your own experience* of the journey that grounds your faith and life and keeps you on the path.

I would encourage you to pick up other books in the series. There is only one destination, but many ways to get there. Not everything in every book will work for you (we are all unique), but in every book you will find much to help you discover your own path on the journey to the One in whom we all "live and move and have our being" (Acts 17:28)

May all be well with you on the journey
Henry F. French, Series Editor

PREFACE

Madeleine L'Engle—novelist, poet, Christian essayist and speaker—dared to explore, and with the strength of her piercing insight to illuminate, aspects of the journey with Christ that more timid minds might bypass. An imaginative artist, fully engaged with the world—its beauties and its heartbreaking realities—Madeleine blazed a path of honesty and integrity, sharing her humanness and failures as well as moments of glory and exultation, through her presence in the world (until her death in 2007 at age 88)—and preeminently through her many works of both fiction and nonfiction.

In her Crosswicks Journal series of autobiographical nonfiction books, named after her beloved Connecticut family home, she opened up to readers a world in which a star-gazing rock is a fixture of everyday life—a life in which prayers and Eucharists can be celebrated not only in church sanctuaries, but in living rooms or at sick beds—and in which philosophical and theological reflections among family and friends create as natural a rhythm as common meals and daily chores.

In the pages of Madeleine's many acclaimed books, we are allowed an intimate acquaintance with a soul fully alive to God. She was a remarkable woman who was a longtime wife (of actor Hugh Franklin, d. 1986), a mother of three, and a grandmother and great-grandmother—ever bringing yet another generation of readers into her intriguing domain of imagination and the Spirit.

Madeleine affirmed in no uncertain terms her allegiance to Christ, calling herself "a particular incarnationalist," who pursued life's largest questions through the one specific person of Jesus as her path to understanding God. Yet her widely informed, reflective method was far from the reductionist approaches of those believers she dubbed "fundalits"—literalist fundamentalists who sought to make the gospel manageable by drawing lines around what it is and what it isn't.

For Madeleine, only poetry would suffice (whether in her many probing narrative poems or her novels and essays studded with fresh metaphors and analogies)—along with living life deeply as it came to her in ever-changing surprise, excruciating challenge, and a multiplicity of questions.

Many readers resonate with lines she wrote in her nonfiction book *The Rock That Is Higher*: "We are all strangers in a strange land, longing for home, but not quite knowing what or where home is. We glimpse it sometimes in our dreams, or as we turn a corner, and suddenly there is a strange, sweet familiarity that vanishes almost as soon as it comes."

Yet she found those glimpses eminently worth recording and ruminating on. She wrote in her 1996 book of reflections on icons and idolatry, *Penguins and Golden Calves*: "I struggle to write about God and God's love, knowing that I am totally inadequate, and yet feeling called to proclaim a love so marvelous that it can only be wondered at and rejoiced in with delight."

And so we are blessed with not only Madeleine's wide range of imaginative works, including children's and young adult books such as her 1963 Newbery Award–winning *A Wrinkle in Time*, but also with an "ongoing journal" of her Christian life, recorded in such collections of essays as *The Irrational Season*, *Stone for a Pillow*, and *Walking on Water*.

Drawing from the wisdom of Madeleine's sixty-some titles (including her collections of poetry), we are privileged to share not only her unique and heady engagement with *what is*—but also a taste and a celebration, for like-minded souls, of *what is to come* in a life destined to be lived in God's loving presence.

While this *40-Day Journey with Madeleine L'Engle* can include only selected excerpts from her vast oeuvre, it offers a taste of some of her deepest insights designed to whet the appetite for more. It is an invitation to take the inner journey with Madeleine and to feast with her in praise and affirmation of the God Who Is.

Isabel Anders
Sewanee, Tennessee

How to Use This Book

Your 40-day journey with Madeleine L' Engle gives you the opportunity to be mentored by a great contemporary spiritual writer and Christian leader. The purpose of the journey, however, is not just to gain "head" knowledge about Madeleine L' Engle. Rather, it is to begin living what you learn.

You will probably benefit most by fixing a special time of day in which to "meet with" your spiritual mentor. It is easier to maintain a spiritual practice if you do it regularly at the same time. For many people, morning, while the house is still quiet and before the busyness of the day begins, is a good time. Others will find that the noon hour or before bedtime serves well. We are all unique. Some of us are "morning people" and some of us are not. Do whatever works *for you* to maintain a regular meeting with Madeleine L' Engle. Write it into your calendar and do your best to keep your appointments.

It is best if you complete your 40-day journey in 40 days. A deepening focus and intensity of experience will be the result. However, it is certainly better to complete the journey than to give it up because you can't get it done in 40 days. Indeed, making it a 40- or 20-week journey may better fit your schedule, and it just might be that spending a whole week, or perhaps half a week, reflecting on the reading, the scripture, and the prayers and then practicing what you are learning could be a powerfully transforming experience as well. Again, set a schedule that works for you, only be consistent.

Each day of the journey begins with a reading from Madeleine L' Engle. You will note that the readings, from day to day, build on each other and introduce you to key ideas in her understanding of Christian life and faith. Read each selection slowly, letting the words sink into your consciousness. You may want to read each selection two or three times before moving on, perhaps reading it out loud once.

Following the reading from Madeleine L' Engle's writings, you will find the heading *Biblical Wisdom* and a brief passage from the Bible that relates directly to what she has said. As with the selection from Madeleine L' Engle, read the biblical text slowly, letting the words sink into your consciousness.

Following the biblical reading, you will find the heading *Silence for Meditation.* Here you should take anywhere from five to twenty minutes meditating on the two readings. Begin by getting centered. Sit with your back straight, eyes closed, hands folded in your lap, and breathe slowly and deeply. Remember that breath is a gift of God; it is God's gift of life. Do nothing for two or three minutes other than simply observe your breath. Focus your awareness on the end of your nose. Feel the breath enter through your nostrils and leave through your nostrils.

Once you feel your mind and spirit settling down, open your eyes and read both the daily reading and the biblical text again. Read them slowly, focus on each word or phrase, savor them, explore possible meanings and implications. At the end of each day you will find the heading *Notes.* As you meditate on the readings, jot down any insights that occur to you. Do the readings raise any questions for you? Write them down. Do the readings suggest anything you should do? Write it down.

Stay at it as long as it feels useful. When your mind is ready to move on, close your eyes and observe your breath for a minute or so. Then return to the book and the next heading: *Questions to Ponder.* Here you will find a few pointed questions by Isabel Anders, the book's compiler and editor, on the day's reading. These are general questions intended for all spiritual seekers and communities of faith. Think them through and write your answers (and the implications of your answers for your own life of faith and for your community of faith) in the *Notes* section.

Many of these *Questions to Ponder* are designed to remind us that although spirituality is always personal, it is simultaneously relational and communal. A number of the questions, therefore, apply the relevance of the day's reading to faith communities. Just remember, a faith community may be as large as a regular organized gathering of any religious tradition or as small as a family or the relationship between spiritual friends. You don't need to be a member of a church, synagogue, mosque, or temple to be part of a faith community. Answer the questions in the context of your particular faith community(s).

Then move on to the heading, *Psalm Fragment.* Here you will find a brief verse or two from the Hebrew book of Psalms that relate to the day's reading. The Psalms have always been the mainstay of prayer in the Christian tradition.

Reflect for a moment on the *Psalm Fragment* and then continue on to the heading *Journal Reflections.* Several suggestions for journaling are given that apply the readings to your own personal experience. It is in journaling that the "day" reaches its climax and the potential for transformative change is greatest. It would be best to buy a separate journal rather than use the Notes section of the book. For a journal you can use a spiral-bound or ring-bound notebook or one of the hardcover journal books sold in stationery stores. (See the next section for some suggestions for how to keep a journal.)

The *Questions to Ponder* and *Journal Reflections* exercises are meant to assist you in reflecting on the daily reading and scripture quotations. Do not feel that you have to answer every question. You may choose which questions or exercises are most helpful to you. Sometimes a perfectly appropriate response to a question is "I don't know," or "I'm not sure what I think about that." The important thing is to record your own thoughts and questions.

After *Journal Reflections*, you will find two more headings. The first is *Prayers of Hope & Healing*. Madeleine L'Engle knew well that one of the highest services a Christian can perform is prayer for family and friends, for one's community of faith, for the victims of injustice, and for one's enemies. Under this heading you will find suggestions for prayer that relate to the key points in the day's readings. The last heading (before *Notes*) is *Prayer for Today*, a one- or two-line prayer to end your "appointment" with Madeleine L'Engle and to be prayed from time to time throughout the day.

Hints on Keeping a Journal

A journal is a very helpful tool. Keeping a journal is a form of meditation, a profound way of getting to know yourself—and God—more deeply. Although you could read your 40-day journey book and reflect on it "in your head," writing can help you focus your thoughts, clarify your thinking, and keep a record of your insights, questions, and prayers. Writing is generative: it enables you to have thoughts you would not otherwise have had.

A Few Hints for Journaling

1. Write in your journal with grace. Don't get stuck in trying to do it perfectly. Just write freely. Don't worry about literary style, spelling, or grammar. Your goal is simply to generate thoughts pertinent to your own life and get them down on paper.
2. You may want to begin and end your journaling with prayer. Ask for the guidance and wisdom of the Spirit (and thank God for that guidance and wisdom when you are done).
3. If your journaling takes you in directions that go beyond the journaling questions in your 40-day book, go there. Let the questions encourage, not limit, your writing.
4. Respond honestly. Don't write what you think you're supposed to believe. Write down what you really do believe, insofar as you can identify that. If you don't know, or aren't sure, or if you have questions, record those. Questions are often openings to spiritual growth.
5. Carry your 40-day book and journal around with you every day during your journey (only keep them safe from prying eyes). The 40-day journey process is an intense experience that doesn't stop when you close the book. Your mind and heart and spirit will be engaged all day, and it will be helpful to have your book and journal handy to take notes or make new entries as they occur to you.

Journeying with Others

You can use your 40-day book with a spiritual friend or partner or with a small group. It would be best for each person to first do his or her own reading, reflection, and writing in solitude. Then when you come together, share the insights you have gained from your time alone. Your discussion will probably focus on the Questions to Ponder; however, if the relationship is intimate, you may feel comfortable sharing some of what you have written in your journal. No one, however, should ever be pressured to share anything in their journal if they are not comfortable doing so.

Remember that your goal is to learn from one another, not to argue or to prove that you are right and the other person wrong. Just practice listening and trying to understand why your partner, friend, or colleague thinks as he or she does.

Practicing intercessory prayer together, you will find, will strengthen the spiritual bonds of those who take the journey together. And as you all work to translate insight into action, sharing your experience with each other is a way of encouraging and guiding each other and provides the opportunity to gently correct each other if that becomes necessary.

Continuing the Journey

When the 40 days (or 40 weeks) are over, a milestone has been reached, but the journey needn't end. One goal of the 40-day series is to introduce you to a particular spiritual guide with the hope that, having whet your appetite, you will want to keep the journey going. At the end of the book are some suggestions for further reading that will take you deeper in your journey with your mentor.

WHO WAS MADELEINE L'ENGLE?

When Madeleine L'Engle died at age 88 in 2007, the many readers of her nonfiction, poetry, and fiction for young adults and adults alike were bereft. As Laurel Snyder wrote in a Salon.com column (September 10, 2007): "A sixth grader could follow her logic, embrace her characters, sense the themes of good and evil, man and nature, science and faith, and, without feeling overwhelmed by the book, simply enjoy a good read. But when that sixth grader turned into a seventh, or eighth, or ninth grader, or—God forbid—an adult, she or he might find even more."

It is that "something more"—Madeleine's deep engagement with the great classical questions of life and death, braided with her Christian understanding and commitment—that has made her more than 60 books beloved candidates for study, reading, and rereading by hundreds of thousands of serious seekers through the years.

Madeleine L'Engle Camp, the only child of Madeleine Hall Barnett and Charles Wadsworth Camp, was born in Manhattan on November 29, 1918. Her great-grandmother had also been named Madeleine L'Engle. Besides being the author of the John Newbery Medal–winning young adult novel *A Wrinkle in Time*, which has sold more than eight million copies, Madeleine is known for an entire series of "children's" books with cosmic themes—employing concepts drawn from her study of Einstein and other twentieth-century physicists. It was always her belief that children could grasp concepts such as relativity and quantum reality (such as we can speak of it) that adults often strained to approach.

A Wrinkle in Time was initially rejected by 26 publishers before its acceptance by Farrar, Straus and Giroux. It is now in its 69th printing. *Wrinkle* was followed by *A Wind in the Door*, *A Swiftly Tilting Planet*, *Many Waters*, and *An Acceptable Time*, sequels in the "Time" series. As Laurel Snyder continues: "Remember the cherubim from *A Wind in the Door*? How he insisted on being called a cherubim (instead of a cherub) because he was 'nearly plural'? Remember all his many eyes and wings? That was L'Engle—all eyes and wings, constantly moving. Different things to different people, at different stages of understanding. A million surfaces, all of them true."

This artistic complexity, matched by her smooth lucidity, carries over into L'Engle's many books of Christian reflections—a multivolume journal of her "real life" with examples taken from her fictional works and mixed in to produce levels upon levels. In the self-revealing pages of these journals, we find deep meditations on the vocation of being a storyteller; the nature of truth; the limits of "reality"; and what can be required of us toward each other and in relation to God along the way.

The very titles of these nonfiction autobiographical works illustrate the strength of her grounding in biblical story: *Stone for a Pillow*, *Walking on Water*, *The Rock That Is Higher*. And within her writings on the Christian life, her transcendent vision (and what one critic calls "a peculiar splendor" in her style) has delighted readers of all ages, at various stages of doubt or belief, especially those searching for like-minded company on the journey.

In the process of my selecting representative quotes from Madeleine's diverse body of work, some clear patterns emerged. What might be termed "supernatural" to some minds is to Madeleine a part of the great unknown universe—but not off-limits to our imaginations, and even our habitation, through the growth of our spirits.

A quote from her beloved novel *A Ring of Endless Light* illustrates the sort of connection she frequently is able to make between the world of untapped transcendence and that of our own Christian walk:

> "Prayer was never meant to be magic," Mother said.
> "Then why bother with it?" Suzy scowled.
> "Because it's an act of love," Mother said.

I was privileged to have met and studied under Madeleine when she lectured and taught in Chicago in the 1970s, and to have been honored by her writing an introduction to and endorsement of my first book, *Awaiting the Child: An Advent Journal* (Cowley Publications, 1987, 2005). In it she wrote: "St. John of the Cross says that in the evening of life we shall be judged on love; not on our accomplishments, not on our successes and failures in the worldly sense, but solely on love."

Madeleine walked this journey herself, leaving us her personal legacy as a witness to the "million surfaces" of the Christian life, accessible in varying degrees to any who also take this journey. Seeking not only a life of *prayer and reflection and love*, but also one of *maturity*, is the overriding theme of these pages—as her quotes express the fine distinctions that a soul must deal with in the exigencies of life.

She once pointed out in an interview:

> In the funeral service in the Book of Common Prayer these words are said: "Remember thy servant, O Lord, according to the favor which thou bearest upon thy people, and grant that, increasing in knowledge and love of thee, he may go from strength to strength, in the life of perfect service." I believe that. Our identity, our self, our soul, goes on growing to a deeper fullness in love of God, leading us toward the kind of maturity God planned for us in the first place. For now, that is all I need to know.

Madeleine L'Engle
November 29, 1918—September 6, 2007

40-DAY

Journey

Ash Wednesday

Journey

Day 1

2/25/09

TWO PHOTOGRAPHS OF TWO VERY separate and different people. . . have within them more than they are in themselves; in them I glimpse, for at least a fragment of a second, the forgiveness of God.

The Greeks, as usual, had a word for the forgiving kind of love which never excludes. They call it agape. . . . Agape means "a profound concern for the welfare of another <u>without</u> any desire to control that other, to be thanked by that other, or to enjoy the process."

Not easy. But if we can follow it, it will mean that we will <u>never</u> <u>exclude</u>. Not the old, the ill, the dying. Not the people who have hurt us, who have done us wrong. Or the people to whom we have done wrong. Or our children. . . . It teaches me not only about <u>forgiveness</u> but about how to hope to give guidance without manipulation.

❧

BIBLICAL WISDOM

Then Peter came and said to him, "Lord, if another member of the church sins against me, how often should I forgive? As many as seven times?" Jesus said to him, "Not seven times, but, I tell you, seventy-seven times." Matthew 18:21-22

SILENCE FOR MEDITATION

QUESTIONS TO PONDER

- Madeleine L'Engle describes *agape* as a love that never excludes. Why is *inclusion* so important to the nature of love? *acceptance*
- How do we sometimes use lesser definitions of "love" to seek to control and manipulate others? *want to fix - may not B broken*
- Jesus set the standard for forgiveness higher than we normally do. What does his teaching on forgiveness require of us, and how can we begin to practice *agape* toward all others, especially in our faith community?

Psalm Fragment

Happy are those whose transgression is forgiven,
whose sin is covered.
Happy are those to whom the LORD imputes no iniquity,
and in whose spirit there is no deceit. Psalm 32:1-2

Journal Reflections

- As you begin your 40-day journey with Madeleine L'Engle, jot down remembrances of times when you have felt, "for at least a fragment of a second, the forgiveness of God."
- Consider and describe in a paragraph any "unfinished business" in your current relationships, and how mutual forgiveness, in the light of God's love for you and others, can bring healing in each instance.
- Make a list of ways to practice *agape* through practical acts of kindness and love this week. Include thanksgiving for these opportunities in your prayers.

Prayers of Hope & Healing

Thank God for the actual pictures or snapshots in your mind of those who remind you of God's love and forgiveness; pray that you might remain connected, be renewed in relationships, or become reconnected in spirit with them.

Prayer for Today

Almighty, forgiving God, help me to accept your healing love today and to practice forgiveness in my daily walk with you and others. Amen.

Notes

to recognize that we are each already forgiven - thanks to the sacrifice of Jesus to truly believe, only then do we forgive

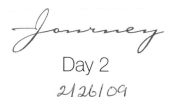

Day 2

2/26/09

GOD, THROUGH THE ANGEL GABRIEL, called on Mary to do what, in the world's eyes, is impossible, and instead of saying, "I can't," she replied immediately, "Be it unto me according to thy Word."

God is always calling on us to do the impossible. It helps me to remember that anything Jesus did during his life here on earth is something we should be able to do, too.

When spring-fed Dog Pond warms up enough for swimming . . . I often go there in the late afternoon. Sometimes I will sit on a sun-warmed rock to dry, and think of Peter walking across the water to meet Jesus. As long as he didn't remember that we human beings have forgotten how to walk on water, he was able to do it.

If Jesus of Nazareth was God become truly man for us, as I believe he was, then we should be able to walk on water, to heal the sick, even to accept the Father's answer to our prayers when it is not the answer that we hope for, when it is *No.* Jesus begged in anguish that he be spared the bitter cup, and then humbly added, "but not as I will. Father, as you will."

In art, either as creators or participators, we are helped to remember some of the glorious things we have forgotten, and some of the terrible things we are asked to endure, we who are children of God by adoption and grace.

. . . The chief job of the teacher is to help us to remember all that we have forgotten. . . . One of the great sorrows which came to human beings when Adam and Eve left the Garden was the loss of memory, memory of all that God's children are meant to be. Perhaps one day I will remember how to walk across Dog Pond.

BIBLICAL WISDOM

[Jesus] said to them, ". . . For truly I tell you, if you have faith the size of a mustard seed, you will say to this mountain, 'Move from here to there,' and it will move; and nothing will be impossible for you." Matthew 17:20

Silence for Meditation

Questions to Ponder

- When has something "impossible" been required of you that God enabled you to do? What was the outcome?
- How can we *know* when our human will is aligned with God's will as we pray, "Your will be done"? Why is it important that we pray this prayer together in our worship?
- What specifically do you think we as humans have "forgotten" about our true nature, our relationship with God, and our ability to live as Jesus lived?

Psalm Fragment

For you have delivered my soul from death,
and my feet from falling,
so that I may walk before God
in the light of life. Psalm 56:13

Journal Reflections

- What is *your* impossible task—your "walking on Dog Pond"? If you have several, record them in your journal today.
- Think of times when you could identify with Peter in his doubts and when you have found yourself "sinking." How did this feel? What brought you back up "above the surface"?
- Reflect on how Jesus, our teacher, shows us all how to live in the glorious freedom of the children of God. What does this freedom mean to you?

Prayers of Hope & Healing

Ask God for continued help in learning Jesus' way and for the opportunity to bring others along with you on this path.

Prayer for Today

God of all wonders, teach us the "glorious impossible" in our own lives, as we give you all the glory and praise, in Jesus' name. Amen.

Notes

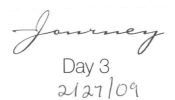

Day 3

2/27/09

WE HAVE FALSE EXPECTATIONS OF our holy days, of our churches, of each other. We have false expectations of our friends. Jesus did not. He had expectations, but they were not false, and when they were not met, he did not fall apart. He was never taken in by golden calves!

Friendship not only takes time, it takes a willingness to drop false expectations, of ourselves, of each other. Friends—or lovers—are not always available to each other. Inner turmoils can cause us to be unhearing when someone needs us, to need to receive understanding when we should be giving understanding.

BIBLICAL WISDOM

Little children, let us love, not in word or speech, but in truth and action.
1 John 3:18

SILENCE FOR MEDITATION

QUESTIONS TO PONDER

- What false expectations do we sometimes harbor—of our church, our friends, and those who minister to us daily? In what specific ways do we need to adjust our expectations?
- What are the "golden calves"—the idols—in our lives that may threaten to distract us from our walk with God?
- Are we willing to take time for true, soul friendship in order to touch those in our lives who are needy or seeking answers? If so, how will we do so this week? If not, why not?

PSALM FRAGMENT

The Lord is near to all who call on him,
to all who call on him in truth. Psalm 145:18

Journal Reflections

- Think about several "cries for help" you may have heard so far this week. How did you (or will you) respond?
- Make a prayer list in your journal and add the names of those you know to be in need. Ask God to show you whether you are to take any action in these specific situations.
- In what ways do you feel *understood? Misunderstood?* Are you known as a person of compassion who *understands* others?

Prayers of Hope & Healing

Pray for clarity and a stilling of turmoil in your own heart, for true "connection" with other souls you encounter, and for increased perception of how the Spirit is working in all your lives.

Prayer for Today

Lord, bring hope to your needy children today, including me. Teach us the way of understanding. Amen.

Notes

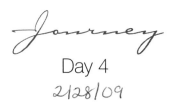
Day 4
2/28/09

As I READ THE OLD and New Testaments I am struck by the awareness therein of our lives being connected with cosmic powers, angels and archangels, heavenly principalities and powers, and the groaning of creation. It's too radical, too uncontrolled for many of us, so we build churches which are the safest possible places in which to escape God.

We pin [Jesus] down, far more painfully than he was nailed to the cross, so that he is rational and comprehensible and like us, and even more unreal. And that won't do. That will not get me through death and danger and pain, nor life and freedom and joy.

⌐

BIBLICAL WISDOM

For in him all things in heaven and on earth were created, things visible and invisible, whether thrones or dominions or rulers or powers—all things have been created through him and for him. Colossians 1:16

SILENCE FOR MEDITATION

QUESTIONS TO PONDER

- How does our culture either encourage or discourage our awareness that we are connected to cosmic powers? How might such an awareness affect our prayers? Our decision making? Our relationships?
- In what ways might church programs and duties actually enable us to escape from God? How can we avoid this "trap"?
- How is the cross irrational? Does our own taking up of the cross "make sense"? In what ways do you believe taking up the cross can lead to freedom and joy?

PSALM FRAGMENT

For who in the skies can be compared to the LORD?
Who among the heavenly beings is like the LORD? Psalm 89:6

JOURNAL REFLECTIONS

- Consider ways in which certain of your *activities or relationships* may get in the way of quiet times of meditation with Jesus. Any changes suggested?
- Write a prayer asking God to reveal *attitudes* that can block your relationship with God and with others in your community of faith.
- In what ways do you participate in the "groaning of creation" through your vocation and your Christian life of faith?

PRAYERS OF HOPE & HEALING

Pray for all who feel alienated from God and wish to find evidence in the world of God's love and care.

PRAYER FOR TODAY

Father of our Lord Jesus Christ, bless our efforts and join our hearts both in church and out of church, that we may find you ever near us, to heal and to help, to the glory of your name. Amen.

NOTES

Day 5

3/1/09

"You mean you're comparing our lives to a sonnet? A strict form, but freedom within it?"

"Yes," Mrs. Whatsit said. "You're given the form, but you have to write the sonnet yourself. What you say is completely up to you."

—Mrs. Whatsit to Calvin in *A Wrinkle in Time*

&

Biblical Wisdom

Work out your own salvation with fear and trembling; for it is God who is at work in you, enabling you both to will and to work for his good pleasure. Philippians 2:12b-13

Silence for Meditation

Questions to Ponder

- In regard to her novel *A Wrinkle in Time*, Madeleine L'Engle often pointed out that, because it was too difficult for adults to understand, it was labeled a children's book. In the light of Mrs. Whatsit's pronouncement, does the paradox of Philippians 2:12b-13 make sense to you? Why or why not?
- If you are a "sonnet," what truth are you expressing through your "lines"?
- In what ways do you feel God working through your human effort and prayers as you create your "sonnet"? How does your personal expression of God relate to the network of relationships that you experience in the Spirit?

Psalm Fragment

My flesh and my heart may fail,
 but God is the strength of my heart and my portion forever. Psalm 73:26

Journal Reflections

- Write about what it means to you to "work out your own salvation with fear and trembling" in the knowledge that "God is at work in you."
- Write a sonnet or other short poem that expresses your devotion to God and your purpose in serving God. OR find another person's words that accurately reflect the depth of your own heart's response and copy them in your journal.
- The cross brings together God's love toward us and our efforts to "work out" our relationship to Christ here on earth. In what (if any) ways does the symbol of the cross help you in understanding your journey? How is your life defined by the cross?

Prayers of Hope & Healing

Pray for a deeper experience of how God is working in your life and the lives of those closely connected to you.

Prayer for Today

God, let my life sweetly sing of your truth and be an expression of beauty to the world. Amen.

Notes

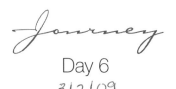

Day 6
3/2/09

JOHN OF KRONSTADT, A RUSSIAN priest of the nineteenth century, counseled his penitents to take their sins of omission and commission, when they get too heavy, and hang them on the cross. I find this extremely helpful. . . .

Sometimes when I hang on the cross something which is too heavy for me, I think of it as being rather like the laundry lines under our apple trees, when I have changed all the sheets in the house. The wind blows through them, the sun shines on them, and when I fold them and bring them in in the evening they smell clean and pure.

If I could not hang my sins on the cross I might tend to withdraw, to refuse responsibility because I might fail. . . .

BIBLICAL WISDOM

For the message about the cross is foolishness to those who are perishing, but to us who are being saved it is the power of God. 1 Corinthians 1:18

SILENCE FOR MEDITATION

QUESTIONS TO PONDER

- How does it feel to you to "hang on the cross" those things in your life that are too heavy to bear? In what ways might a community of faith help you to do this?
- How does God renew us when we are open to the wind of the Spirit and the sunlight of love? What does this "refreshing" enable us to do?
- What is our own responsibility when we claim the release of sins and the freeing experience of Jesus' cross? How can our being "set free" also free others around us?

Psalm Fragment

From the womb of the morning,
like dew, your youth will come to you. Psalm 110:3

Journal Reflections

- Bring before God both your sins of omission and your sins of commission in your prayers this week. Imaginatively hang them on the cross. Write about the experience.
- List ways in which God's "foolishness" overshadows any of the world's wisdom for you.
- Imagine other visual images of surrendering your sins to Christ. Describe "rituals of release" you might use to let go of your sins and failings to the mercy of Christ.

Prayers of Hope & Healing

Pray for yourself and others in your circle of family and friends, that you may experience the freedom of forgiveness and the joy of a renewed life.

Prayer for Today

Lord, make me clean and fresh within, that my life may reflect your work and your love. Amen.

Notes

Day 7

3/3/09

BACH IS, FOR ME, THE Christian artist *par excellence*, and if I ask myself why, I think it has something to do with his sense of newness. I've been working on his C Minor Toccata and Fugue since college, and I find something new in it every day. And perhaps this is because God was new for Bach every day, was never taken for granted. Too often we do take God for granted.

❧

BIBLICAL WISDOM

Do your best to present yourself to God as one approved by him, a worker who has no need to be ashamed, rightly explaining the word of truth. 2 Timothy 2:15

SILENCE FOR MEDITATION

QUESTIONS TO PONDER

- What practices and disciplines can we offer to God over and over, day after day, year after year? How can a community of faith help us develop these practices?
- If we find that we are taking our spiritual life for granted, what can we do to "wake ourselves up"? How can spiritual friendships provide balance and correction to our walk with God?
- Recall times that God's patience with you has kept you in the paths of faithfulness in your life. What is your response to God's faithful love?

PSALM FRAGMENT

One thing I asked of the LORD,
that will I seek after:
to live in the house of the LORD
all the days of my life,
to behold the beauty of the LORD,
and to inquire in his temple. Psalm 27:4

Journal Reflections

- Write about your own skills and creativity. Dedicate your skills and creativity to God and write about ways in which using them well is an expression of thanksgiving to God.
- How has God rewarded you or shown you the fruit of your labor when pursuing your spiritual path? What effect does your spirituality have on other people of faith? On those who do not have faith?
- Write about times when you felt yourself taking God for granted. How did you become aware of this? How did you respond? What spiritual practices or spiritual friendships help you not to take God and faith for granted?

Prayers of Hope & Healing

Pray for an intentional walk with God, seeking the Lord in the beauty of holiness in all your worship, private and corporate.

Prayer for Today

Dear God, reveal to me your loveliness through the wonders of this created world, as you help me also to be a co-creator myself. Amen.

Notes

car broke down

Journey

Day 8
3/4/09

THE MARVELOUS THING IS THAT . . . holiness is nothing we can earn. We don't become holy by acquiring merit badges and Brownie points. It has nothing to do with virtue or job descriptions or morality. It is nothing we can *do*, in this do-it-yourself world. It is gift, sheer gift, waiting there to be recognized and received. We do not have to be qualified to be holy. We do not have to be qualified to be whole, or healed.

⌁

BIBLICAL WISDOM

We know that a person is justified not by the works of the law but through faith in Jesus Christ. And we have come to believe in Christ Jesus, so that we might be justified by faith in Christ, and not by doing the works of the law, because no one will be justified by the works of the law. Galatians 2:16

SILENCE FOR MEDITATION

QUESTIONS TO PONDER

- Why is holiness always a gift rather than an effort on our part?
- Is there *any* sense in which the Christian life *is* a "do-it-yourself" endeavor? What is the relationship between works and faith?
- How has God's saving grace been experienced in your own life and history? What roles have the community of faith and spiritual friendships played in your experience of grace?

PSALM FRAGMENT

Wash me thoroughly from my iniquity,
and cleanse me from my sin. Psalm 51:2

Journal Reflections

- How do you experience the relation between "holiness" and "wholeness"? Draw a diagram if it aids understanding. What actions and attitudes help you to connect these two concepts?
- How has God healed you from your past and shown you your own spiritual worth? In what ways does this experience lead you to spread healing love to those around you?
- How does God's "sheer gift" of grace to you move you to respond in your relationships with others? Make a list of ways you can serve others out of gratitude to God this week.

Prayers of Hope & Healing

Pray for a continued sense of healing and renewal through the days ahead on this journey, for yourself and all others.

Prayer for Today

Thank you, Lord, for your holiness that gives us back to ourselves with the wholeness you intended us to have.

Notes

Day 9
3/5/09

THERE AREN'T ANY EASY ANSWERS to the questions being raised today, and it may be too easy for me to remember Jesus saying, *"Greater love has no man than to give up his life for his friend. . . ."*

Sacrifice is no longer popular, but I think that sometimes it can lead to true joy. Even the simplest of unions does not come free. There is always sacrifice.

⌐

BIBLICAL WISDOM

Whoever does not take up the cross and follow me is not worthy of me.
Matthew 10:38

SILENCE FOR MEDITATION

QUESTIONS TO PONDER

- In what particular ways and through which specific people has Jesus' love as the Ideal Friend been revealed to you? How does your community of faith talk about sacrifice?
- As Madeleine L'Engle notes: "Sacrifice is no longer popular." In what ways does our culture discourage sacrifice and encourage self-gratification? How can a community of faith counter this cultural tendency?
- In what ways might willing sacrifice lead to deeper joy and meaning in life? What mentors and spiritual friends have especially taught you about sacrifice? How?

PSALM FRAGMENT

Offer right sacrifices,
and put your trust in the LORD. Psalm 4:5

Journal Reflections

- What does it mean to you to "take up your cross and follow" Jesus?
- Reflect on the people around you. What are specific ways in which you can sacrifice for the sake of another, here and now—not for personal gain, but because truth and goodness require it?
- Write a short meditation on the role of mutual sacrifice in your interpersonal relationships.

Prayers of Hope & Healing

Pray for wisdom to know when true sacrifice is required, and is not an undue punishing of yourself with no spiritual gain.

Prayer for Today

All-loving God, accept my sacrifice of thanksgiving, and teach me to walk in the way of your cross, embracing both its demands and its joys. Amen.

Notes

Journey

Day 10
3 / 6 / 09

THE BEST WAY TO HELP the world is to start by loving each other, not blandly, blindly, but realistically, with understanding and forbearance and forgiveness.

⁓

BIBLICAL WISDOM

One of them, a lawyer, asked him a question to test him. "Teacher, which commandment in the law is the greatest?" He said to him, " 'You shall love the Lord your God with all your heart, and with all your soul, and with all your mind.' This is the greatest and first commandment. And a second is like it: 'You shall love your neighbor as yourself.' On these two commandments hang all the law and the prophets." Matthew 22:35-40

SILENCE FOR MEDITATION

QUESTIONS TO PONDER

- Madeleine wrote the above admonition in her 1997 New Year's letter to friends around the world. What do you think she means by realistic love? Is it what Jesus meant when he said to "love your neighbor as yourself"?
- What are the results for ourselves and others when we act toward them "blandly" and "blindly"? What is the "understanding" that Madeleine calls for? How might such understanding shape our action?
- Why do "forbearance and forgiveness" always need to be a part of the "formula" for love?

PSALM FRAGMENT

But let all who take refuge in you rejoice;
*   let them ever sing for joy.*
Spread your protection over them,
*   so that those who love your name may exult in you.* Psalm 5:11

JOURNAL REFLECTIONS

- God is our refuge and strength—especially when we are living in love toward our neighbor. Write about what that means to you.
- Who are the people in your life whom you are called to love realistically and with understanding? How might you begin to grow in realistic and understanding love for them?
- Write in your journal a letter to your loved ones that expresses your understanding of Jesus' commandment that fulfills "all the law and the prophets." Let your heart teach you the words. If it seems right, share your letter with those you are writing to.

PRAYERS OF HOPE & HEALING

Pray for discernment in your treatment of others and for purity of spirit as you seek to love God with all your heart and mind and strength.

PRAYER FOR TODAY

Dear God, help me to love today, not blandly or blindly, but with a heart that is open to you and your commandments. Amen.

NOTES

Journey

Day 11

3 / 7 / 09

AFTER ANNUNCIATION

This is the irrational season
When love blooms bright and wild.
Had Mary been filled with reason
There'd have been no room for the child.

~

BIBLICAL WISDOM

Then Mary said, "Here am I, the servant of the Lord; let it be with me according to your word." Then the angel departed from her. Luke 1:38 *true faith*

SILENCE FOR MEDITATION

QUESTIONS TO PONDER
time to let go of my life, ego, strained relationships
- What do you perceive that God is asking of you at this time in your life?
  What are the signs in your life that point to the opening up of *revelation* or
  leading toward some action or acceptance? *everything falling apart*
- What "reasons" have been overcome or overshadowed in your life when
  God opened up another way? How does the biblical pattern of Mary's
  acceptance of the "glorious impossible" set an example for us in our own
  walk with God? *'let it be w/me according to your word'*
- When a moment of unusual God-awareness passes—when "the angel
  departs"—what helps you keep believing in the validity of your experience?
  How would you describe your faith in this process to others in your believing community? *gradual, steady process of trust*

PSALM FRAGMENT

Let your work be manifest to your servants,
    and your glorious power to their children. Psalm 90:16

Journal Reflections

- Record some of the promises of God that seem "irrational" to the strictly reasoning mind. How does each one open us up to God's glorious power? In what ways have you experienced this in your life?
- How does your faith community's worship participate in the "irrational"— in this and every liturgical season? How would you explain these practices and beliefs to someone outside your circle of faith? *to care for Gods children*
- What does it mean to you to be God's servant in our world and time? How are you called to follow Mary's pattern of acceptance? What aspects of Christ are you being called to bear forth into the world? *- to have faith, trust in the Lord's guidence, trust that he will care for me*

Prayers of Hope & Healing

Pray for a deeper understanding of the ways in which God calls us in our ordinary lives, and how cooperation with God makes the impossible manifest.

Prayer for Today

God of all glory, open my heart and my life to all aspects of your divine revelation, that my heart may respond: "Let it be with me according to your word." Amen.

Notes

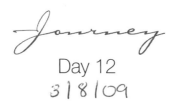

Day 12

3 | 8 | 09

AS CHRISTIANS WE ARE NOT meant to be less human than other people, but _more_ human, just as Jesus of Nazareth was _more_ human.

One time I was talking to Canon Tallis, who is my spiritual director as well as my friend, and I was deeply grieved about something, and I kept telling him how woefully I had failed someone I loved, failed totally, otherwise that person couldn't have done the wrong that was so destructive. Finally he looked at me and said calmly, "Who are you to think you are better than our Lord? After all, he was singularly unsuccessful with a great many people."

That remark, made to me many years ago, has stood me in good stead, time and again. I have to try, but I do not have to succeed. Following Christ has nothing to do with success as the world sees success. It has to do with love. *try w/ best intentions from love*

BIBLICAL WISDOM

I do not understand my own actions. For I do not do what I want, but I do the very thing I hate. Romans 7:15

SILENCE FOR MEDITATION

QUESTIONS TO PONDER

b/c we are lead by care + love, we love God, for others, beyond our own egos

- What do you think it means for Christians to be "more human" than other people? How has God used your willingness to be "more human" to bring others to faith? *by example* *it's not worth it*
- Why do we often fall into difficulty when we try to succeed at all costs? What would "being more human" mean in these situations?
- If even the apostle Paul could not avoid doing the very things he intended _not_ to do, what does this imply about forgiving ourselves for our own humanness? How do the others in your community help you to grow "more human" in the context of the Christian life as you live it together? *example*
holding me accountable

PSALM FRAGMENT

Create in me a clean heart, O God,
and put a new and right spirit within me. Psalm 51:10

JOURNAL REFLECTIONS

- List ten ways in which Jesus appeared not to "succeed" with the people he encountered in his ministry. What was the real situation in each case?
- How have your own "failures" in the past led to deeper waters of commitment and understanding in your Christian life? Be specific in recounting the lessons learned from failure for yourself and for those whom your life touches in your community.
- What are some concrete expressions of love that you are being called to carry out in your life right now? How will your attitude toward success and failure inform your attempts to love?

PRAYERS OF HOPE & HEALING

Pray for an openness and an honesty with God, in your meditations and your prayers, that will allow you to be "more human" with yourself, with God, and with others you encounter.

PRAYER FOR TODAY

Lord of love, may your Spirit cleanse my heart of all doubt and fear, and renew me in my dedication as your human servant. Amen.

NOTES

[handwritten: Danielle's Birthday]

Journey

Day 13
[handwritten: 3/9/09]

THE GODS WE ERECT ARE easier to worship than the Creator of the universe. They're more comprehensible. The God I believe in is not comprehensible in finite, mortal terms. God is infinite, immortal, all-knowing. I have a point of view, you have a point of view. But God has *view.* But we don't like having to depend on that which we cannot control, manipu- *[handwritten: big picture]* late, dominate. *[handwritten: ,, blind faith]*

BIBLICAL WISDOM

Ever since the creation of the world [God's] eternal power and divine nature, invisible though they are, have been understood and seen through the things he has made. Romans 1:20

SILENCE FOR MEDITATION

[handwritten: companionship, approval, stuff, money]

QUESTIONS TO PONDER

- What are the "gods we erect" in our lives that vie for attention and worship and can turn us from the eternal God? *[handwritten: chasing worldly pleasures]*
- Madeleine says that "God has *view.*" What does this mean for us as we struggle to know and follow the truth to the best of our ability in the world? *[handwritten: God knows past, future]*
- What evidence do you see in the natural world of God's immortal, all-knowing, infinite power? What does it teach us about living in love as a community of faith and goodness, despite what the world does to us? *[handwritten: ocean, sky, leaves, birds, animals, how plants grow]*

PSALM FRAGMENT *[handwritten: the power of love]*

Praise him, sun and moon;
  praise him, all you shining stars! Psalm 148:3

Journal Reflections *allowing God's love to flow through me*

- What are you seeking from God right now? Be specific in terms of your hopes and desires, sincerely asking for God's guidance in all of these matters. *not to judge, be present / listen / giving from my heart*
- *yeah* How have you tried to manipulate, control, or dominate the events and outcomes that you desire in life? What might God be calling you to relinquish in terms of control and certainty at this time? Why? *trust / faith*
- How do the disciplines of the Christian life, individual practices and community worship patterns, serve to direct your will toward God? What practices of your tradition are you especially called to work on in this journey? *small group, worship band, Sunday brunch, Cov Brd prayer life*

Prayers of Hope & Healing *caring / giving*

Pray for healing of both attitude and perspective so that you are able more fully to "let go and let God."

Prayer for Today

God of creation, may my voice and my life praise you as do the sun and the moon, the stars, the earth, and all creatures that live. Amen.

Notes

Journey

Day 14
3/10/09

IN A SENSE, PRAYING AND writing involve the same disciplines. When I sit down with an act of will, either before the typewriter or to pray, I have to let go of my control and listen. I listen to the story or I try to get beyond the words of prayer and listen to God. Ultimately when I hear, that is the gift, not my act of will, not my act of virtue. It is pure gift. I guess my favorite analogy for the difference between faith and works came from Rudolf Serkin. My husband and I heard him play Beethoven's *Appassionata* Sonata better than Beethoven could play it. When the last note faded away there wasn't a sound. Then, slowly, like the ocean waves, the applause swelled. Later I realized that we had been present at a moment of transcendence, of transfiguration. What did Serkin have to do with that? He practices eight hours a day every day. I have to write every day whether I want to or not. I have to pray every day whether I want to or not. It's not a matter of feeling like it, or waiting until I feel inspired, because both in work and in prayer, inspiration comes during rather than before. *help me to remain inspired / help me to live passionately — make it matter for the sake of the Lord, in his & honor — fervid delight in discipline of discipleship — live for the Lord —*

BIBLICAL WISDOM

Therefore, my beloved, be steadfast, immovable, always excelling in the work of the Lord, because you know that in the Lord your labor is not in vain.
1 Corinthians 15:58

SILENCE FOR MEDITATION

QUESTIONS TO PONDER

- What is the relationship, as you see it, between day-to-day discipline and the experience of "transcendence, transfiguration"? *recognition*
- In what ways are we to be "immovable," and in what ways must we remain flexible in our Christian walk? How do these principles apply in our relationships with our fellow believers? *unretractable, unwavering faith — flexible enough to hear God's will, even love the unloveable... there are many!*

- Why do you think inspiration comes "during rather than before" our best efforts at work and prayer? How have you experienced this phenomenon in your own life? *Inspiration seeks opportunity — by reading the words of the Lord, we may just hear*

PSALM FRAGMENT *something we've needed to hear*

For the word of the LORD is upright,
and all his work is done in faithfulness. Psalm 33:1-4

JOURNAL REFLECTIONS

- List the spiritual disciplines or practices in your life that need to be strengthened and made more regular in order for you to keep growing. How will you do this? *praying always / reading daily / listen*
- When has your experience of God and God's gifts transcended your highest expectations? What lessons did you learn from this experience?
- What gifts from God are you especially thankful for in your life? How will you use them responsibly in the days ahead? *Communication — I pray to be more open, listen more attentively*

PRAYERS OF HOPE & HEALING

Pray for awareness of all that God gives, in every area of life, and ask to be a wise steward of all these gifts. *Gratitude in my attitude too blessed to be stressed*

PRAYER FOR TODAY

Lord, may we worship you in true faithfulness as you quicken and enliven us in your service. Amen.

NOTES

Journey

Day 15
3/12/09

PHARAOH'S CROSS

It would be easier to be an atheist; it is the simple way out.
But each time I turn toward that wide and welcoming door
it slams in my face, and I—like my forbears—Adam, Eve—
am left outside the garden of reason and limited,
chill science and the arguments of intellect.
Who is this wild cherubim who whirls the flaming sword
'twixt the door to the house of atheism and me?

⁓

BIBLICAL WISDOM

You must make every effort to support your faith with goodness, and goodness with knowledge. . . . 2 Peter 1:5

SILENCE FOR MEDITATION

QUESTIONS TO PONDER

- Why are the arguments of intellect not enough to guide our lives? Have you ever felt "left outside the garden of reason . . . and the arguments of intellect"? How does faith transcend reason in your experience?
- In what ways does God's goodness permeate our resistance to the ways of God and make way for divine love in our lives? What role does doubt play in our journey with God?
- How does goodness support knowledge, and vice versa? How do both give you assurance in your faith—as an individual and within your wider community of belief?

PSALM FRAGMENT

Be still, and know that I am God!
    I am exalted among the nations,
    I am exalted in the earth. Psalm 46:10

Journal Reflections

- Write five honest doubts you have about religion or spirituality or faith or God and address them to God in a sincere, seeking spirit. What answers do you receive as you seek for guidance at this stage of your journey of faith? *why am I afraid to trust, let my old life go, turn over prob*
- What will it require in your life right now to "be still" and know God's presence in a new way? What will you cease to do? What work or discipline will you take on? *hold fam, in love, trust in future - peace/calm*
- What lessons does the world of nature teach you about God's presence and ongoing creation? What is the "flaming sword" in your life that keeps you from sinking into unbelief? *church family / Howie & Renie*

Prayers of Hope & Healing

Pray for an airing of honest doubts that will cleanse your spirit and allow God to do a new thing in your life. *create a right spirit in me oh lord*

Prayer for Today

God of grace and glory, I come to you even in my doubts and weaknesses and thank you that you *are* and that you hear my prayer. Amen.

thank you for your faithfulness

Notes

Journey

Day 16
3/12/09

THE MOMENT THAT HUMILITY BECOMES self-conscious, it becomes hubris. One cannot be humble and aware of oneself at the same time. Therefore, the act of creating—painting a picture, singing a song, writing a story—is a humble act? This was a new thought to me. Humility is throwing oneself away in complete concentration on something or someone else. *agree w/ putting ego aside / selfless*

BIBLICAL WISDOM

Finally, all of you, have unity of spirit, sympathy, love for one another, a tender heart, and a humble mind. 1 Peter 3:8

SILENCE FOR MEDITATION

QUESTIONS TO PONDER

give credit where credit is due ... remember God's grace

- If thinking about oneself and one's "humility" immediately changes humility to hubris, how might the virtue of humility be approached? If we cannot judge our own humility, how can we develop this trait?
- What other activities besides the ones mentioned in the above quote—"painting a picture, singing a song, writing a story"—can serve to pull one's concentration completely away from "self"? When have you experienced this phenomenon? *yoga, meditation, nature walks*
- When we do not allow ourselves to "get in the way" and are concentrating on a task by "throwing ourselves away," how does this bring us closer to God and to others? What specifically can you learn from this experience?

self wants acknowledgement + praise

PSALM FRAGMENT

[The LORD] leads the humble in what is right,
and teaches the humble his way. Psalm 25:9

JOURNAL REFLECTIONS *MLK, JFK, Dali Lama*

- Think of models of humility you have known, people in history and those living today. What do you think was (is) the secret of their selflessness?
- Write a list of qualities that complete the sentence: *Humility is . . .* Across from this, write a list of actions or attitudes of which it can be said: *Humility is not . . .*
- Can prayer and meditation also qualify as "creative acts" that involve throwing ourselves away, forgetting ourselves, and abandoning ourselves to God? Why or why not? How do the tasks of "making" and "creating" in your life teach you about the qualities of true prayer?

PRAYERS OF HOPE & HEALING

Pray for purity of heart, for single-mindedness both in work and in prayer—not only on this 40-day journey, but increasingly in your life with God.

PRAYER FOR TODAY

God of all creativity, show me your face so that I lose myself in your love and splendor. Amen.

NOTES

Thank you that this day I have the wisdom, by your grace, to take time to ☺ nuture my spirit, read your work + yoga

FIRE BY FIRE

My son goes down in the orchard to incinerate
Burning the day's trash, the accumulation
Of old letters, empty toilet-paper rolls, a paper plate,
Marketing lists, discarded manuscript, on occasion
Used cartons of bird seed, dog biscuit. The fire
Rises and sinks; he stirs the ashes till the flames expire.

Burn, too, old sins, bedraggled virtues, tarnished
Dreams, remembered unrealities, the gross
Should-haves, would-haves, the unvarnished
Errors of the day, burn, burn the loss
Of intentions, recurring failures, turn
Them all to ash. Incinerate the dross. Burn. Burn.

 ↝

BIBLICAL WISDOM

And forgive us our sins,
*   for we ourselves forgive everyone indebted to us.*
And do not bring us to the time of trial. Luke 11:4

SILENCE FOR MEDITATION

QUESTIONS TO PONDER

- Why is it necessary to "clean house" spiritually as well as in our actual homes? What spiritual disciplines are equivalent to a bonfire for discarded objects?
- The image of fire illustrates how such acts can both purify and destroy at the same time. Why are both results important? How might spiritual housecleaning help you to begin life anew? How might a community of faith help individuals with such housecleaning?

- How might your own faith community conduct a "housecleaning" and a "bonfire" corporately, for the good of its own spiritual health? What would be your part in this endeavor?

PSALM FRAGMENT

Do not remember the sins of my youth or my transgressions;
according to your steadfast love remember me,
for your goodness' sake, O LORD! Psalm 25:7

JOURNAL REFLECTIONS

- Write out a "to burn" list in your journal and ask God for guidance in how to go about constructing a "spiritual bonfire."
- Why does the Lord's Prayer specify that in order to be forgiven we must also forgive those people who are indebted to us? Write in your journal what this means to you in the context of your present circle of relationships.
- How do you decide what attitudes and actions are hindering you in your journey with God? What criteria enable you to make the lists of those things that must "burn"?

PRAYERS OF HOPE & HEALING

Agree to God's "cleaning up" in your life, even though the losses that are entailed may cause you pain and grief.

PRAYER FOR TODAY

Dear Lord, may the burning of the old make way for the new in my life with you, and may I be enabled to recognize beauty from ashes in the process. Amen.

NOTES

'Let go'

Journey

Day 18
3|14|09

I AM A PARTICULAR INCARNATIONALIST. I believe that we can understand cosmic questions only through particulars. I can understand God only through one specific particular, the incarnation of Jesus of Nazareth. This is the ultimate particular, which gives me my understanding of the Creator and of the beauty of life. I believe that God loved us so much that he came to us as a human being, as one of us, to show us his love.

~

BIBLICAL WISDOM

For God so loved the world that he gave his only Son, so that everyone who believes in him may not perish but may have eternal life. John 3:16

SILENCE FOR MEDITATION

QUESTIONS TO PONDER

- What do you think Madeleine means when she specifies that she is "a particular incarnationalist"?
- As an artist, Madeleine sees God's hand in all creation; but the Way to God appears to her ultimately in Jesus. Ponder why this incarnation of God in the man Jesus is at the center of our Christian faith.
- What are the implications for the significance of our own lives that *God dwelt in human form here on earth in Jesus the Son?*

PSALM FRAGMENT

But I call upon God,
and the LORD will save me. Psalm 55:16

JOURNAL REFLECTIONS

- Describe your belief in one sentence. What understanding of Jesus and his life is most central to your faith?

- How does God continue to "save you" through Jesus as you journey your own path and live out your own stories? Record the times at which God's "saving action" was especially poignant and redirecting in your life, listing dates if possible.
- What evidences of God's love give you hope and keep you on your faith journey today? What part do other believers play in helping you maintain this inner belief and hope?

PRAYERS OF HOPE & HEALING

Pray for a deeper understanding of the salvation that God has freely given us in Jesus Christ and that we may all learn how to share this core truth more effectively.

PRAYER FOR TODAY

God of salvation, bestow on me healing strength, deeper understanding, and continued perseverance in my walk with you and others. Amen.

NOTES

Liz & Nick / last Sunday

Journey

Day 19
3 | 15 | 09

"WHEN WE FALL, AS WE always do, we pick ourselves up and start again. And when our trust is betrayed the only response that is not destructive is to trust again. Not stupidly, you understand, but fully aware of the facts, we still have to trust."

—Dr. Austin in *The Young Unicorns*

⌁

BIBLICAL WISDOM

Now may the Lord Jesus Christ himself and God our Father, who loved us and through grace gave us eternal comfort and good hope, comfort your hearts and strengthen them in every good work and word. 2 Thessalonians 2:16-17

SILENCE FOR MEDITATION

We're imperfect we're bound to fail - can't define us! LEARN

QUESTIONS TO PONDER

- Why is it important when we fall down in our spiritual journeys to "pick ourselves up and start again"? When have you had this experience of needing to start over and not give up? *Peaks + valleys/stops + starts*
- When our trust is betrayed by another person, Madeleine says that we have two choices and that one of them is inherently destructive. We can close ourselves off from believing or trusting in anyone else again; or we can allow ourselves to have failed in whatever way, to be human, and to begin to learn to trust anew. Why is it so important spiritually to "get back on the bicycle" and start pedaling again? *negativity impedes faith journey*
like eating rat poison
- Madeleine's words also underline the importance of reason in this process. "Not stupidly, you understand." We are to keep our thinking channels open, to remain fully aware of the facts—and then to let go again. How do reason and faith act as "dance partners" in your life with Christ and with others? *through faith + trust - trust in ourselves to learn, to love - no matter WHAT the other does!*

PSALM FRAGMENT

In God, whose word I praise,
in God I trust; I am not afraid;
what can flesh do to me? Psalm 56:4

JOURNAL REFLECTIONS

- List in your journal several instances when you have had to trust in the face of failure or loss, when you have had to get back on the bicycle again. How did God restore your trust, and what was the outcome? *Michael*
- Make a list of those in your faith community who are at a crossroads of deciding whether or not to continue after failure and loss. Lift their names to God as you give thanks for your own "falls" and what they have taught you. *Uncle + Mickey.*
- Why is it important to continue in "every good work and word" toward others around you, even as you stumble and fail in your own life? Where do you get the strength and courage to do this? *faith + trust in the Lord*

PRAYERS OF HOPE & HEALING *+ be alright;*

Pray for understanding and forgiveness toward yourself for failing, as well as toward those who may have harmed you or caused you to fall.

PRAYER FOR TODAY

God of the second—and third—chance, I praise you for your love, your forgiveness, your strength to help me begin anew this day. Amen.

May I learn to forgive as I've been forgiven

NOTES

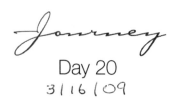

Day 20
3 / 16 / 09

IT DOESN'T WORK IF I think of God as Out There. . . . Back when it was still possible to believe that this planet was the center of everything, that the sun and the moon and the stars were hung in the sky entirely for our benefit, it was quite possible to think of God as our Maker, Out There. . . . We have too often thought of God as being *outside* the universe, creating us, and looking at what happened to us, concerned, but Out There. But as I contemplate the vastness of the night sky on a clear, cold night, God Out There does not work. Out There is *too* far out. God becomes too remote. . . . Scripturally, God is always in and part of Creation; walking and talking with Adam and Eve, taking Abraham out to see the stars, wrestling with Jacob. And, in the most glorious possible demonstration of God *in* and *part of* Creation, God came to us in Jesus of Nazareth, fully participating in our human birth and life and death and offering us the glory of Easter.

༄

BIBLICAL WISDOM

Now to God who is able to strengthen you according to my gospel and the proclamation of Jesus Christ, according to the revelation of the mystery that was kept secret for long ages. . . . Romans 16:25

SILENCE FOR MEDITATION

QUESTIONS TO PONDER

- Why does it matter so much that God is here with us in Christ, and not just "Out There"? What does it tell us about our place in the universe?
- In what ways do you experience God in and through the creation?
- How is Jesus Christ the culmination of "the mystery that was kept secret for long ages"?

Psalm Fragment

The heavens are yours, the earth also is yours;
the world and all that is in it—you have founded them. Psalm 89:11

Journal Reflections

- Consider the three examples Madeleine gives of God's walking and talking with Adam and Eve, showing Abraham the stars, and wrestling with Jacob. Have you had similar experiences of God being present with you? If so, write about them in your journal. What was the experience like? What did you learn?
- How do the human birth, life, and death of Jesus of Nazareth help us to seek and find the God of the universe?
- Study Jesus' own words in the Gospels concerning his Father, and then write in your journal three "principles of relationship" that can apply to us as well in our relationship to Christ.

Prayers of Hope & Healing

Pray for continued understanding of how God comes to us in Christ, and for the peace and assurance we can have in our walk with the Lord and with others.

Prayer for Today

God of the cosmos, of all earthly life, and author of the resurrection, I praise you with my human voice, joining with angels and archangels to proclaim your glory.

Notes

Journey

Day 21
3/11/09

As I run over my favorite characters in both Old and New Testaments, I can't find one who was in any worldly way qualified to do the job which was nevertheless accomplished; Moses was past middle age when God called him to lead his children out of Egypt, and he spoke with a stutter. He was reluctant and unwilling and he couldn't control his temper. But he saw the bush that burned and was not consumed. He spoke with God in the cloud on Mount Sinai, and afterwards his face glowed with such brilliant light that the people could not bear to look at him.

In a very real sense not one of us is qualified, but it seems that God continually chooses the most unqualified to do his work, to bear his glory. If we are qualified, we tend to think that we have done the job ourselves. If we are forced to accept our evident lack of qualification, then there's no danger that we will confuse God's work with our own, or God's glory with our own.

~

Biblical Wisdom *praise*

Those who speak on their own seek their own glory; but the one who seeks the glory of him who sent him is true, and there is nothing false in him. John 7:18

Silence for Meditation

Questions to Ponder

- Who are your favorite Bible characters? How were they initially unequipped to carry out God's will?
- How do you understand the word *glory*? Why is it crucial that we "give God glory" in all that we do, or attempt to accomplish? How can we do this in practical ways?
- Do you think of yourself as competent? self-disciplined? of average skill? or generally unqualified for the tasks you have been given? How has God revealed to you your true abilities and strengths?

Psalm Fragment

Ascribe to the LORD the glory of his name;
worship the LORD in holy splendor. Psalm 29:2

Journal Reflections

- What are your equivalents of Moses' "stutter" that you might be tempted to use as excuses for not proceeding in your spiritual calling? Make a list of your "weaknesses" and a parallel column of your "strengths" in your journal. Ponder how God is turning your weaknesses into strengths.
- Have you ever congratulated yourself on achieving a particular outcome and then later found out how much of your experience was truly *grace* and *gift* from God (and others)? If so, write about the experience. If not, write about your awareness of how God and others participate in your "success."
- Write about the ways in which you have experienced yourself as someone chosen to "bear God's glory." What does this divine "choosing" mean to you?

Prayers of Hope & Healing

Pray for a revealing of God's greatness, beauty, love, forgiveness, and guidance—all aspects of God's glory—in your own life and in that of your community of faith.   *who God is*

Prayer for Today

Lord of hope and might, show me both my value in your eyes *and* my dependence on you to accomplish anything at all. Amen.

Notes

Glory - being at the top
- Gods creation / nature / music

Journey

Day 22
3 / 18 / 09

EPIPHANY

Unclench your fists, *shoulders, mind-open hands*
Hold out your hands.
Take mine.
Let us hold each other.
Thus is his Glory
Manifest.

⌁

BIBLICAL WISDOM

For where two or three are gathered in my name, I am there among them.
Matthew 18:20

SILENCE FOR MEDITATION

QUESTIONS TO PONDER

- How we shape and hold our hands in each other's presence can be an indication of how we are treating each other. In what other ways can we shut others out besides revealing clenched fists? *crossing arms / frown*
- In what circumstances in your community do you most experience Christ among you? *reaching out to help one another*
- What other "epiphanies" (sudden revelations of the divine) in your life—such as experiencing the beauty and wonder of nature—bring you closer to God? How are other people a part of that revealing as well? *talking*

PSALM FRAGMENT

Let the righteous rejoice in the LORD
and take refuge in him.
Let all the upright in heart glory. Psalm 64:10

Journal Reflections

- What recent encounters with other people have served to reveal God's glory to you? Describe these experiences. *How is*
- Make a list of (or draw) the various ways in which hand positions signify spiritual truths: for example, open palms to receive the gifts of the Spirit. Draw as many hands as needed!
- Consider the many ways that Jesus used his hands: to touch and heal, to wash his disciples' feet, to bear the nails of the cross, to bless his disciples with peace in his post-resurrection appearances. Now consider your own hands and what they can accomplish. Write about how you use (or could use) your hands both in service to the world God loves and as a sign of God's glory.

Prayers of Hope & Healing

Pray for a coming together of any who may be estranged in your community or from you personally—that hands will reach out to hands, and hearts to hearts.

Prayer for Today

Dear God, Creator of my body, my hands, my heart—anoint me in your service that I may be swift to do your will. Amen.

Notes

sudden revelations

Journey

Day 23

~~3/19/09~~
3/23/09

No matter how deep the faith, we each have to walk the lonesome valley; we each have to walk it all alone. The world tempts us to draw back, tempts us to believe we will not have to take this test. We are tempted to try to <u>avoid</u> not only our own suffering, but that of our fellow human beings, the <u>suffering of the world</u>, which is part of our own suffering. But if we draw back from it (and we are free to do so), [Franz] Kafka reminds us that "it may be that this very holding back is the one evil you could have avoided." [Any discipline] involves participation in suffering, in the ills and the occasional stabbing joys that come from being <u>part</u> of the <u>human drama</u>. *temporary condition*

Biblical Wisdom

I consider that the sufferings of this present time are not worth comparing with the glory about to be revealed to us. Romans 8:18

Silence for Meditation

Questions to Ponder *finding peace amid challenges*

- What is your "lonesome valley" right now? In what ways do you perceive that God is with you as you walk through it? Where is your community of faith in your "lonesome valley"? *w/ me — people placed in my path*
- How are suffering and glory intertwined, according to Romans 8:18? Why does it never work simply to seek to avoid suffering in our lives? *10*
- How does awareness of suffering in the rest of the world affect our relationship to God? How does it challenge our faith?
  may wonder why God allows injustice

Psalm Fragment

O Lord . . . you are the one who lifts me up from the gates of death. Psalm 9:13

Journal Reflections

- When has God lifted you from "the gates of death"? Write a short prayer of thanksgiving that takes into account both the suffering and the "stabbing joys" you may have experienced.
- What has made you most aware of the ways that we are connected in our earthly journey? What practical steps can you take to help alleviate suffering in the world around you, locally or globally?
- Is "holding back" from suffering blocking your progress in your spiritual path, as Kafka suggests? How can you avoid that "one evil"? What assurances does God give that you are equipped to go forward? List some Bible verses that assure you of this.

Prayers of Hope & Healing

Pray for courage for yourself and those close to you in *not shrinking from suffering*, but pressing on, armed with God's strength.

Prayer for Today

God of glory, I affirm my trust in your goodness even in the straits that threaten to undo me. My hope remains in you. Amen.

Notes

Journey

Day 24
3/24/09

THROUGH NO VIRTUE OF OUR own we are made dead to the old and alive in the new.

And for each one of us there is a special gift, the way in which we may best serve and please the Lord whose love is so overflowing. And gifts should never be thought of quantitatively. One of the holiest women I have ever known did little with her life in terms of worldly success; her gift was that of bringing laughter with her wherever she went, no matter how dark or grievous the occasion. Wherever she was, holy laughter was present to heal and redeem.

In the Koran it is written, "He deserves Paradise who makes his companions laugh."

BIBLICAL WISDOM

I will turn their mourning into joy,
I will comfort them, and give them gladness for sorrow. Jeremiah 31:13

listen / care

SILENCE FOR MEDITATION

dead to old life
old virtues QUESTIONS TO PONDER reborn to life
w/ God in christ

- What does it mean to be "dead to the old and alive in the new"? How does Christ accomplish this? Think of specific times when you have experienced such rejuvenation in your life. when I feel I make a difference
- What are the particular gifts you have been given that enable you to serve God by serving the world God loves? How are you called to exercise them, and which ones are being called into service right now?
- Consider the virtue of *holiness*: How does our single-mindedness or purity of heart relate to our gifts? Why is it important to affirm and *agree to* our own gifts in order to use them effectively? acknowledge Gods gifts to us for others / serving - Gods will

PSALM FRAGMENT

You have turned my mourning into dancing;
you have taken off my sackcloth
and clothed me with joy. Psalm 30:11

JOURNAL REFLECTIONS

- Think about people who have shared their gifts with you through the years. Write down their names and something about what they gave you. How did each help to further your journey with Christ?
- Write about the place of laughter in this "vale of tears" in which suffering is also ever-present. Reflect on the relationship between gladness and sorrow as two sides of the same coin in your life and in the experiences of your community.
- Make a list of things you can do this week to lighten someone's load and perhaps share the gift of laughter. *Traci ... listen*

PRAYERS OF HOPE & HEALING

Pray for an easing of burdens, a sense of lightness and trust that is as much a gift of God as a serious thoughtfulness can be.

PRAYER FOR TODAY

O God, turn my mourning into rejoicing and my sorrow into lasting joy, for the sake of your Son, Jesus Christ. Amen.

NOTES

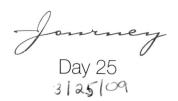

Day 25

3/25/09

DURING MY JOURNEY THROUGH LIFE I have moved in and out of agnosticism and even atheism, as I become bewildered by what mankind has done to God; and so, too often, I see God in man's image, rather than the other way around. But I cannot live for long in this dead-end world, but return to the more open places of my child's intuitive love of God, where I know that all creatures are the concern of the God who created the galaxies, and who nevertheless notes the fall of each sparrow. And from the darkness I cry out: God!

BIBLICAL WISDOM

Since we are God's offspring, we ought not to think that the deity is like gold, or silver, or stone, an image formed by the art and imagination of mortals. Acts 17:29

SILENCE FOR MEDITATION

QUESTIONS TO PONDER

- How does the world around us try to put God in humanity's image? How has this affected your faith journey?
- What does it mean to live as people created in *God's* image and likeness? How can such understanding—and our consequent actions—help to renew "this dead-end world"?
- How would our spiritual lives be altered if we were able to return to a childlike acceptance and love of God? What do you think is preventing this from happening—and spreading? Be specific.

PSALM FRAGMENT

As for me, I shall behold your face in righteousness;
when I awake I shall be satisfied, beholding your likeness. Psalm 17:15

JOURNAL REFLECTIONS *Creator* *Redeemer*

- What are your favorite word pictures of God: Shepherd, Rock, Door, King, Mother Hen, Lamb, Father, or . . . ? How is God both described by these metaphors and totally beyond all of them for you? Use some of these images in your prayers and envision the attributes of God that speak to you through them.
- How does assurance of God's care for the last and the least among us— helpless children and sparrows—serve to strengthen your own trust in God's existence and love for us?
- What worship practices in your individual and community life bring you closest to God and build up your faith most effectively? How can you increase your participation in those practices?

PRAYERS OF HOPE & HEALING

Pray for an honesty that consists of both doubt and belief, two sides of the human "coin" that can hold us in creative and dynamic relationship with our great God.

PRAYER FOR TODAY

Lord I believe; help my unbelief. Amen.

NOTES

God's thoughts / desire - discernment how do we know that / when we're following God's will vs our own

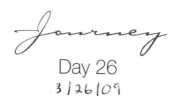

Day 26

3/26/09

WHEN I THINK OF THE incredible, incomprehensible sweep of creation above me, I have the strange reaction of feeling fully alive. Rather than feeling lost and unimportant and meaningless, set against galaxies which go beyond the reach of the furthest telescopes, I feel that my life has meaning. Perhaps I should feel insignificant, but instead I feel a soaring in my heart that the God who could create all this—and out of nothing—can still count the hairs of my head.

BIBLICAL WISDOM

But even the hairs of your head are all counted. Do not be afraid; you are of more value than many sparrows. Luke 12:7

SILENCE FOR MEDITATION

QUESTIONS TO PONDER

- What makes you feel fully alive? How is God part of that experience for you?
- What activities and relationships involving other people also contribute to your sense of meaningfulness and well-being in the world? How are these experiences also a tribute to God's creation?
- Why does it matter that God is intimately concerned with our human lives? How will we treat our own bodies and those of others in this light?

PSALM FRAGMENT

[God] is mindful of his covenant forever,
of the word that he commanded, for a thousand generations. Psalm 105:8

Journal Reflections

- Search out three facts we now know about the universe that will stretch your mind and challenge your spirit. Write them in your journal. Pray this week with a special awareness of this vastness and infinite scope of God's care.
- How do *you* experience God's faithfulness to the divine covenant with humans as it comes down even to our generation? What is your part in this covenant?
- How should humans treat the rest of creation in the light of God's infinite love for all creation? What are three practical ways in which you can express your commitment to love the creation that God loves?

Prayers of Hope & Healing

Pray for an expansion of your own vision to include and value all that God has created, including yourself; and ask for particular ways in which you can share this consciousness with your faith community.

Prayer for Today

God of stars and sparrows, mountains and galaxies, come among us and show me your glory; exquisitely remind me of your love. Amen.

Notes

Journey

Day 27
3/27/09

THE ENFLESHING OF THE WORD which spoke the galaxies made the death of that Word inevitable. All flesh is mortal, and the flesh assumed by the Word was no exception in mortal terms. So the birth of the Creator in human flesh and human time was an event as shattering and terrible as the eschaton. If I accept this birth I must accept God's love, and this is pain as well as joy because God's love, as I am coming to understand it, is not like man's love.

Which one of us can understand a love so great that we would willingly limit our unlimitedness, put the flesh of mortality over our immortality, accept all the pain and grief of humanity, submit to betrayal by that humanity, be killed by it, and die a total failure (in human terms) on a common cross between two thieves?

↝

BIBLICAL WISDOM

But God proves his love for us in that while we still were sinners Christ died for us. Romans 5:8

SILENCE FOR MEDITATION

QUESTIONS TO PONDER

- We are all beloved of God, while being mortal. How does the paradox of God's love for us tell us something of God's nature? In what small ways does our own love "reach down"?
- How would you describe the difference between God's love and human love?
- Why is it important that God loved us while we still were sinners? How does this make us feel about becoming whole and becoming clearer mirrors of God's love?

Psalm Fragment

*What are human beings that you are mindful of them,
mortals that you care for them?* Psalm 8:4

Journal Reflections

- List five ways in which God's love reaches down to you from the height of heaven. *protection ; comfort, loving grace , faith , compassion*
- Think of the many ways in which God shows love for you; write about them in your journal and mention them in your prayers this week as revealed blessings toward you. *fellowship /opportunities*
- Draw a diagram of the cross and write words or draw symbols around it that signify what Christ's life, death, and resurrection have accomplished in your life. *gratitude*

God wants to understand our human struggles

Prayers of Hope & Healing

Pray for deeper understanding and thankfulness for God's love in Christ that has brought us into fellowship with God and each other.

Prayer for Today

Lord Jesus Christ, have mercy on me and forgive me my lack of mindfulness of all that you have done. Amen.

Notes

Lenten brunch
Renie

Journey

Day 28
3/28/09

blind faith

GOD EXPECTS US TO BELIEVE—NOT so much in the unbelievable as in the unprovable, that which leads us into the glorious love of God. . . . God's love . . . surrounds us in all we do and at all times unless we reject it, or limit it. Even then, I suspect it is still all around us, but we have blinded ourselves to it. The Holy Spirit has come to help us to understand—the Comforter Jesus promised to send to us.

BIBLICAL WISDOM

And we are witnesses to these things, and so is the Holy Spirit whom God has given to those who obey him. Acts 5:32

SILENCE FOR MEDITATION

QUESTIONS TO PONDER

- How many "unprovable" things can you list that you believe in in your everyday life? How and why must we "suspend disbelief" in order to have faith in God? *we accept the lord w/ trust + faith*
- Do you think we more often live in the security of God's love or "limit" God by our unbelief? Explain. *too gd . to be true / unworthy*
- How have you experienced the presence and comfort of the Holy Spirit in your life? Give specific examples. *comforted when Andy ill Holy Spirit guides on faith journey*

PSALM FRAGMENT

Do not cast me away from your presence,
*   and do not take your holy spirit from me.* Psalm 51:11

JOURNAL REFLECTIONS

- Make a list of current crises and needs both in your life and relationships and in the larger world. Now draw a circle around them that represents God's loving presence that surrounds us in all conditions and at all times.

mom
c. kids
work
pressure
traci

- What symbols of the Holy Spirit speak to you most meaningfully? Why?
- In what ways might you sometimes reject or limit God's love for you? Any thoughts about how to live more faithfully in and through God's love?

accepting the full scope of God's love & grace / lack of

PRAYERS OF HOPE & HEALING *faith in myself*

Pray that the circle of inclusion that is God's love and care will ever extend until it encompasses the whole world.

PRAYER FOR TODAY

Holy Spirit, guide and sustain me in my life in Christ, that I may know more fully the matchless love of Father, Son, and Comforter. Amen.

NOTES

So grateful for the many awesome & faithful people that I've found along my faith journey. Thank you for time this morning w/ the beautiful women in our church family ♡

Journey

Day 29

Mon 3/30

WE MUST WANT TO BE changed by Jesus' marvelous act of loving, Christ willing to be Jesus, to live for us, to show us how to be human, to die for us, to rise from the grave for us, to ascend to heaven for us, to send us the Holy Spirit—and all for love. How splendid! It is so splendid that it cannot be understood by our finite minds alone; it cannot be understood literally. Literalism is death to Christianity. . . . The story is far, far greater than that. It is the truth we live by. It is glory!

و

BIBLICAL WISDOM

How great . . . are the riches of the glory of this mystery, which is Christ in you, the hope of glory. Colossians 1:27

SILENCE FOR MEDITATION

QUESTIONS TO PONDER
to care for one another

- In what specific ways did Jesus show us how to be human? What are the human characteristics of Jesus that make him most accessible to us on our journey? *his understanding of human struggles & temptations*
- How is "literalism" a danger and, as Madeleine points out, "a death" to true Christianity? How do Jesus' teachings lead us beyond a stark literalism to the wholeness of "kingdom thinking"?
- Madeleine's observation that "we must want to be changed by Jesus' marvelous act of loving" is true of both individuals and institutions. How might "Jesus' marvelous act of loving" change institutional churches if they were truly willing to be changed?

PSALM FRAGMENT

O LORD, our Sovereign,
    how majestic is your name in all the earth! Psalm 8:1

- What are the "riches" of Christ for you? How do you experience them? How do they impact, shape, guide your life and relationships?
- Our own story converges with Jesus' story as we contemplate his human life and the love that is brought down through the ages in him. If you were to meet Jesus in our world today, what do you think that encounter would be like? Write your thoughts and a description of what you imagine.
- God's name is "splendid" and a focus of the Holy for Christians. Find five scripture verses that celebrate God's name and incorporate them into your prayers this week. If possible, share this meditation with a group of fellow believers.

PRAYERS OF HOPE & HEALING

Pray for increased understanding and wholeness as you immerse yourself in contemplation of Christ's acts of redemption for us.

PRAYER FOR TODAY

Lord of glory and splendor, enlighten my mind and open my eyes to behold the mystery of your salvation. Amen.

relationship   NOTES

Day 30

Tues 3/31

MARY, THE THEOTOKOS, WAS NOT a success. The most spectacular thing she did was to say *yes* to the angel, an incredible response of courage and faith. She carried this extraordinarily conceived baby and she went, not to her mother, but to her cousin Elizabeth. . . . Mary was young enough to accept the impossible. We tend to limit ourselves to the possible as we grow older. If Mary had the courage to take the impossible into her body, can we not have the courage to take it into our hearts?

she saw the gift / responded without hesitation
an honor

BIBLICAL WISDOM

Now the birth of Jesus the Messiah took place in this way. When his mother Mary had been engaged to Joseph, but before they lived together, she was found to be with child from the Holy Spirit. Matthew 1:18 *Joseph had doubts*

SILENCE FOR MEDITATION

QUESTIONS TO PONDER

- Madeleine calls Mary, Jesus' mother, *Theotokos* (literally *God-bearer*; also *Mother of God*, the one who bore God into the world). Reflect on Mary's response to God. In what ways might both individuals and communities of faith be *Theotokos* or *God-bearers* in our world? *Believe — faith*
- How do we become "young enough" to accept the impossible? In what ways does the innocence of youth make room for the inclusion of God and God's purposes? How can we ourselves return to such an honest openness of heart?
- What might we be shutting out that God wants to bestow on us because we think it impossible? How can we incorporate into our lives the gift of Mary's openness to God? *Stop judging / accept w/ faith*
ways to reach people in need. Opportunities to make
PSALM FRAGMENT *a difference*

All the paths of the LORD are steadfast love and faithfulness,
  for those who keep his covenant and his decrees. Psalm 25:10

JOURNAL REFLECTIONS

- Think deeply about the concept of faithfulness. What would true loyalty and faithfulness require in your life at this time? Be specific.
- What should a servant of the Lord look like? Sound like? In what specific servant-role do you find yourself? Describe its nature.
- Elizabeth was an older mother, and Mary a young one. List some of the advantages of age, and then youth, in learning acceptance of God's gifts to us. What sort of courage is required of the old? Of the young?

PRAYERS OF HOPE & HEALING

Pray for all of the people in your faith community, the old, the young, and those in between. Ask for courage to embody Christ in your own life at your current stage of growth and maturity. *stop judging, love completely acceptance, comfort*

PRAYER FOR TODAY

God of the impossible, be born among us in our lack of faith, our shortsightedness, and our fears. Teach me to open my heart and my life to you as Mary did. Amen.

NOTES

faithfulness: let the cares & responsibilities of this life melt away. become accountable to God first & foremost. place needs of others first of worries about wordly tasks - make more time

servant of the lord - NO FROWNS, posture upright, open body language, good listener, helper

age is patient, grateful - youth excited, energetic

'old age ain't no place for sissies'

youth questions guidance

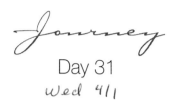

Day 31

Wed 4/1

ALL OF US, ONE WITH God, one with Christ, one with each other. We begin to get an idea of what this means when we think of the body of Christ, and that we are each part of it, each an essential part; there is no part too small or too unworthy or too unimportant to be unnecessary! But it goes further than that.

. . . To love one another as Jesus loved us. As Christ loves us. Can we do it? Can we love one another as Christ loves us? We have to. It isn't going to be any easier than trying to understand the Ascension, or the coming of the Spirit in tongues of flame at Pentecost.

᷍

BIBLICAL WISDOM

[Jesus said,]: "I give you a new commandment, that you love one another. Just as I have loved you, you also should love one another. By this everyone will know that you are my disciples, if you have love for one another." John 13:34-35

SILENCE FOR MEDITATION

QUESTIONS TO PONDER

- Why would Jesus ask such a difficult thing of us: to love each other as he loves us? How is his earthly life an example of this selfless love?
- Madeleine compares the difficulty of keeping the "love commandment" to the difficulty of understanding the deep doctrines of our faith. Which is harder for you? Why? *unconditional love is difficult*
- How does Jesus' principle of the unity of believers in him and in God play out in your own faith community? What particular challenges are you currently facing in achieving this unity?

PSALM FRAGMENT

For your steadfast love is before my eyes,
and I walk in faithfulness to you. Psalm 26:3

Journal Reflections

- What "members" of the body of Christ seem "small" or insignificant to you? Compose a prayer that confesses this. Pray to have eyes to see the importance of everyone and every role that is worked out in the life of the church, and of your own local congregation or group.
- Write a short meditation in your journal on what it means to love others as Jesus loved us.
- In your journal, write a description of yourself as a "disciple" of Jesus. Are you happy with the description? Why or why not?

Prayers of Hope & Healing

Pray for a spirit of unity to grow among your family, friends, coworkers, and fellow worshipers in the days ahead, so that together you may mirror God's steadfast love.

Prayer for Today

Lord and Father of all, I thank you that I am knit together in the body of Christ. Help me to live and love and enable your body in the world. Amen.

Notes

body of Christ / The Church - who is small?
each one of us, each is significant
ea. does what they can - we must
assume ea. doing the best they can
at any given time w/ situations - we
are all fighting our own battles

'Lord, hear my prayer - help me to look deeply enough to
see the light within ea of us. Lift up each member'
' If my concern is truly for others, God will ease my burden
& care for my needs- fill me w/ faith in God's Grace.

Journey

Day 32
Thur 4/2

GOD <u>ALMOST</u> ALWAYS ASKS <u>THE</u> impossible. If it is possible, if it is easy, we can almost always be sure that it is the Tempter asking, not God. God asked Abraham to leave his comfortable home, long after retirement age, go to a strange land with his wife, who was long past childbearing years, and start a family. He asked Gideon to free his captured people from a vast enemy, far more powerful than the little group of Jews hiding in the mountains. He asked the prophets <u>not</u> to foretell the future, but to tell the people where they were, right then, where they had gone wrong, where they had stopped listening to the God of Love, and how they had become, most of them, far more secular than we are in our secular cities today. And he asked Mary to give birth to Jesus who was going to save us from ourselves and our sins.

And Jesus? What did God ask of Jesus . . . ? Jesus was God, for starters. . . . We believe that Christ, the Second Person of the Trinity, left the Godhead to come to us.

༊

BIBLICAL WISDOM

Let the same mind be in you that was in Christ Jesus,
who, though he was in the form of God,
did not regard equality with God
as something to be exploited,
but emptied himself,
taking the form of a slave,
being born in human likeness.
And being found in human form,
he humbled himself
and became obedient to the point of death—
even death on a cross. Philippians 2:5-8

SILENCE FOR MEDITATION

Questions to Ponder

- Who are the prophets today who tell us where we have gone wrong and how to turn back to God? What is your relationship to these prophets?
- Does your community of faith have a "prophetic voice"? If so, how does it make that voice heard? If not, how might it begin to get such a voice?
- What would it mean for individual believers and communities of faith to have "the same mind . . . that was in Christ Jesus"?

Psalm Fragment

Come and see what God has done:
he is awesome in his deeds among mortals. Psalm 66:5

Journal Reflections

- Think of a time when God has asked something that seemed humanly impossible of you. How did you know that the prompting was truly "of God"?
- When have choices or situations you've encountered seemed "too easy"? Do you feel that in any of those cases you were being tempted to take the path of least resistance and to move away from God's will? Reflect on the outcome of your actions in those instances.
- Madeleine talks about Jesus "limiting himself" by leaving the Godhead "to come to us." Paul wrote that Jesus "emptied himself." Write a short meditation on what "self-emptying" meant for Jesus and what it might mean for you as a follower of Jesus.

Prayers of Hope & Healing

Pray for a spirit of adventure for yourself and your faith community, that you would trust that wherever God wants to lead you, you can go in the power and presence of God's Spirit.

Prayer for Today

Holy God, when you ask what seems impossible of me, give me the courage to say yes and move out in faith. Amen.

Notes

Day 33

Fri 4/3

LOVE, LIKE JESUS', IS SELDOM easy. When it's easy, it's sentimentality, not love. Love often says *no* when we would like the answer to be *yes*. Jesus did not allow all the people he had cured to follow him as one of his disciples. He told them to stay where they were and spread the word of love, and often they were disbelieved. He didn't let the rich young man come to him, keeping all his riches. Whenever Jesus calls us, something has to be given away. Our self will. Our eagerness to make judgments about other people's sins. Whenever I do that, I can almost hear Jesus telling me to look at my own sins, instead.

～

BIBLICAL WISDOM

Why do you see the speck in your neighbor's eye, but do not notice the log in your own eye? Matthew 7:3

SILENCE FOR MEDITATION

QUESTIONS TO PONDER

- How do you tell the difference between sentimentality and true love?
- What, in your experience, has had to be "given away" in order for you to follow Jesus? *my will, my selfish fears & desires*
- Jesus wouldn't "let the rich young man come to him, keeping all his riches." What are the implications of this for us in our wealthy, consumerist society? *give it away to keep it - true riches*

PSALM FRAGMENT

You guide me with your counsel,
and afterward you will receive me with honor. Psalm 73:24

JOURNAL REFLECTIONS

- Think of instances in your life when love said no rather than yes. How did you respond? What were the results? *family struggles*
- Why is it so difficult to see our own flaws, while we are able to recognize *denial* shortcomings in our neighbors? Write down in your journal descriptions of times when you have been tempted to make a judgment of someone else, and compose a short prayer for that person instead.
- In what specific ways has God recently given you "counsel"? Write down these experiences and the names of people and/or scripture verses that have conveyed this wisdom to you.

PRAYERS OF HOPE & HEALING

Pray for a surrender of self-will to Jesus and his purposes so that you may more effectively serve him in the world.

PRAYER FOR TODAY

Lord, give me eyes to see and ears to hear the truth, that I may be a grown-up disciple who takes responsibility for my life and who encourages and strengthens others in faith. Amen.

NOTES

Family members

Journey

Day 34
Sat 4/4

GOD DID NOT GIVE ANSWERS; God gave himself, to save us, to free us from our sins. When Christ was born as Jesus in a barn in Bethlehem, that tiny baby bore our sins, and he bore them all his life as he grew into manhood. How heavy they must have been during his last weeks on earth when he knew that his dearest friends did not understand him and were going to betray him. How heavy they must have been when he hung on the cross. But for love of us he carried them. How blessed we are in his love!

ↄ

BIBLICAL WISDOM

He himself bore our sins in his body on the cross, so that, free from sins, we might live for righteousness; by his wounds you have been healed. 1 Peter 2:24

SILENCE FOR MEDITATION

QUESTIONS TO PONDER

- The cross represents for us the complete Christian life: a vertical beam that reaches to God, and a horizontal beam that expresses our connectedness to each other as Christians. What does the vertical connection to God currently feel like to you? How about the horizontal connections?
- How is the cross also a great equalizer in our relationships with others?
- How can we learn to "live for righteousness" in this life?

PSALM FRAGMENT

The LORD lives! Blessed be my rock,
and exalted be the God of my salvation. Psalm 18:46

JOURNAL REFLECTIONS

- Make a list of what you have experienced as blessings from God during this past month. Draw pictures or symbols meaningful to you of what you consider to be the greatest blessings from God that you have experienced.
- The quotation from 1 Peter tells us that the wounds of Jesus are for our healing and strength. How have your own wounds particularly helped you to become stronger?
- The cross with all of its many meanings stands at the very heart of Christian faith. Write a prayer that expresses your understanding of and appreciation for Jesus' cross in your life.

PRAYERS OF HOPE & HEALING

Pray for a deeper understanding and investment in Jesus' story of redemption and its implications for us.

PRAYER FOR TODAY

Lord Jesus, you stretched out your arms on the hard wood of the cross for our salvation. Teach us to pattern our lives after your example, to the glory of God the Father.

NOTES

Journey

Day 35
mon 4/6

WHY CAN'T WE REMEMBER THAT Jesus' last commandment was that we should love each other as he loved us? John, in his first epistle, tells us firmly that if we <u>cannot</u> love each other, love the people we know and have seen, we cannot love God <u>whom</u> we have not seen! If we are able truly to love one another, then we will get a <u>glimpse</u> of understanding of the <u>magnificent love of God</u>.

↶

BIBLICAL WISDOM

Those who say, "I love God," and hate their brothers or sisters, are liars; for those who do not love a brother or sister whom they have seen, cannot love God whom they have not seen. 1 John 4:20

SILENCE FOR MEDITATION

QUESTIONS TO PONDER

- We are reminded again that Jesus' last great commandment, his most important instruction to his disciples, was to *love one another.* How does your community of faith express its obedience to Jesus' great commandment? In what ways might it fall short? *intercessory prayers from the heart*
- If love is the heart of Jesus' life and teaching and death, why has there been and is there still so much violence done in the name of God?
- Jesus asks us to love as he loved. Do you think that is possible for us? *No*
  goal — Would he have asked if it wasn't? What radical changes would happen if we embraced such love as our way of life?

PSALM FRAGMENT

My soul thirsts for God,
for the living God.
When shall I come and behold
the face of God? Psalm 42:2

Journal Reflections

- The psalmist's soul "thirsts for God." In what ways do you recognize the thirstiness of your own soul for God? Make a list of these very personal indicators of your soul's thirst in your journal.
- Are there presently any relationships with other people that are hindering or even blocking your relationship with God? Write down what you need to do to restore love to your neighbors with whom you have differences, before experiencing a deeper union with God.
- As both Madeleine and St. John remind us, no one has seen God, but the love of others opens us to God's presence and gives us knowledge of God. Write a short meditation in your journal on how love has been (or might be) your path to God.

Prayers of Hope & Healing

Pray for continued experiences of *loving one another* through this 40-day journey and beyond, and for the circle of love to grow in depth and numbers as Jesus' love is shared ever more widely.

Prayer for Today

God of love and peace, touch my heart this day and show me your face in the faces of others, that I may come and adore you. Amen.

Notes

Thirst for the peace that comes w/ trust + faith
pray to take time/make time for God to be
present in my life - set my anxieties aside to
be present w/ others - to listen, care, to ask
first 'how can I help' understand the
suffering of others, even concerns that seem
very small to me

what here on this earth need I fear?

Journey

Day 36

to err is human
to forgive, divine Jus 4|7

IF I ACCEPT JESUS' HUMANITY as well as his divinity, then I must allow the human Jesus to do things I don't like [such as the cursing of the fig tree]. The Incarnation does mean that God was willing to become mortal for the sake of us mortal creatures, that Infinite Power and Love willingly and lovingly went through every temptation that comes to any one of us. It is a love so astonishing that it can only be rejoiced in, lived by, but never understood. *does compassion grow from understanding*

BIBLICAL WISDOM

For we do not have a high priest who is <u>unable</u> to sympathize with our weak-nesses, but we have one who in every respect <u>has been tested as we are</u>, yet without sin. Hebrews 4:15

SILENCE FOR MEDITATION

QUESTIONS TO PONDER

- Is it important to you that Jesus—through personal experience—is able to *guilt less necessary//love myself* *to love* "sympathize with our weaknesses"? Why or why not? *YES / I seek forgiveness*
- What difference does it make to you that "in every respect [Jesus] has been tested as we are"? *Jesus knows me + its ok / loves me*
- In what ways was Jesus tested in his earthly life? How did he stop short of succumbing to temptation in each instance? *40 d. in dessert, prayer* *time interrupted, wk tirelessly to minister*

PSALM FRAGMENT

man symbiotic in the great creation

You have multiplied, O LORD my God,
your wondrous deeds and your thoughts towards us;
none can compare with you.
Were I to proclaim and tell of them,
they would be more than can be counted. Psalm 40:5

Richly Blessed

JOURNAL REFLECTIONS

- Search the Gospels for some of Jesus' "hard sayings"—sayings that are difficult for you to accept. Copy them into your journal, and then consider how Jesus' love becomes "tough love" in these teachings.
- Make a list of the temptations that you are currently facing. Read through the Gospels for insights in Jesus' teaching for dealing with these temptations. Write a prayer seeking the wisdom and power of the Holy Spirit in resisting.
- The psalmist speaks of God's "wondrous deeds and thoughts towards us." What are they in your experience?

PRAYERS OF HOPE & HEALING

Pray for insight for yourself and your community as you discern God's will for you in the days ahead.

PRAYER FOR TODAY

God of power and might, come among us with fire and wind, love and grace, that I may resist temptation and find peace through Jesus Christ our Lord. Amen.

NOTES

The hardest is the simplist- NOT the easiest; love one another / forgive each - some people don't make it obvious that they wont face anger + judgement dealing w/tough love situations / forget to forgive + try understanding

Journey

Day 37

Wed 4/8

ALL OF THE STORIES THAT Jesus told reveal their deepest meaning if we see them in their chronological context.

I remember yet again that Jesus told stories—stories which were not intended to be literal, but which were to make a point, and I know that my understanding is widened far more by stories than by provable fact. If it's provable, where's the mystery? Where's the faith? What is there to understand?

I am, as ever, grateful that the scriptural protagonists are not virtuous or moral or perfect, but fallible mortals like the rest of us, struggling to understand what God wants of them, and often getting only the merest glimpse of the purpose for which they have been called.

BIBLICAL WISDOM

But there are also many other things that Jesus did; if every one of them were written down, I suppose that the world itself could not contain the books that would be written. John 21:25

SILENCE FOR MEDITATION

QUESTIONS TO PONDER

- Jesus' stories of sheep and shepherds, vines and branches, masters and slaves, fish and coins and leaven, all serve to reveal who he is, who God is, what the kingdom is—yet they are none of those things literally. Why do you think the Gospel parables and other sayings of Jesus do not specifically spell things out for us but leave us to "work on the puzzle" of their meaning? *to develope trust which leads to faith*
- Which biblical character do you most identify with? Why? What do you learn from his or her story?
- In what sense can it be said that Jesus' stories become our stories?
  morals to live by / stories to teach us how

PSALM FRAGMENT

The LORD will fulfill his purpose for me;
your steadfast love, O LORD, endures forever.
Do not forsake the work of your hands. Psalm 138:8

JOURNAL REFLECTIONS

- Choose your favorite story from the Gospels and write in one column the literal meaning; in a parallel column write what you perceive as the spiritual meaning or "mystery solved."
- Experiencing God's purpose for us is closely connected to God's steadfast love, according to Psalm 138. God's purpose cannot be anything other than good for us. Write a short meditation on how you understand God's purpose for your life. In God's love, who are you? What should you be doing? Where are you headed?
- If you were to write the story of God's coming to you, what imagery would you use?

PRAYERS OF HOPE & HEALING

Pray for increased spiritual understanding and love among the community of the redeemed. *Thank you for 6 new members*

PRAYER FOR TODAY

O Lord, do not forsake the work of your hands, this mortal life that I offer to you today. Amen.

NOTES

water from the well / Samaritan woman
Past doesn't exist / living water of life
She went out it faith to praise his name.

My gift to minister to others can only flourish
in the light of the love of the Lord / living water
to nourish the holy spirit within ~ loving soul
May you guide me in all that I do for your glory

pure light, gentle
warm, loving, strong + sure

95

Journey

Day 38

Thur 4/9
Maundy Supper

WHAT I BELIEVE IS SO magnificent, so glorious, that it is beyond finite comprehension. To believe that the universe was created by a purposeful, benign Creator is one thing. To believe that this Creator took on human vesture, accepted death and mortality, was tempted, betrayed, broken, and all for love of us, defies reason. It is so wild that it terrifies some Christians who try to dogmatize their fear by lashing out at other Christians, because a tidy Christianity with all answers given is easier than one which reaches out to the wild wonder of God's love, a love we don't even have to earn.

❧

BIBLICAL WISDOM

And when [Jesus] had given thanks, he broke [the bread] and said, "This is my body that is for you. Do this in remembrance of me." 1 Corinthians 11:24

SILENCE FOR MEDITATION

QUESTIONS TO PONDER

- When we partake of the Eucharist together as Christ's body, we participate in a mystery that is beyond our finite comprehension. How does your acceptance of the consecrated bread and wine bring Jesus into your life? Why is it essential that this rite be performed in community?
- Do you feel more comfortable with a "tidy Christianity" or "one which reaches out to the wild wonder of God's love"? Explain.
- How has this 40-day journey so far taken you beyond "tidy answers" and closer to the "wild wonder of God's love"?

PSALM FRAGMENT

Before the mountains were brought forth,
or ever you had formed the earth and the world,
from everlasting to everlasting you are God. Psalm 90:2

JOURNAL REFLECTIONS

- Think of times that Christians—perhaps in your own group—have opposed each other. How would you mediate with the words of Jesus to bring them together? What verses come to mind? Write them in your journal.
- Why is it important to realize that none of us has all the answers to what is true Christianity? Make a list of the questions you still have for which you want to ask God for illumination or resolution.
- What answers to prayer have you seen in these weeks?

PRAYERS OF HOPE & HEALING

Pray for appreciation of God's Word, of the Holy Sacrament, of each other, and of how Christ the Word comes to us in community.

PRAYER FOR TODAY

Lord Jesus, be near to us in the breaking of bread. Ignite our hearts with your matchless love. Amen.

NOTES

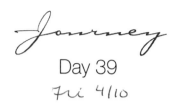

Day 39

Fri 4/10

WE STRUGGLE TO UNDERSTAND, SOMETIMES beyond reason. I have a friend who berates herself for her lack of understanding, and I cry out, "But if you could understand it all, you'd be God!" I cry that to myself, too. We can understand far more than we do, but complete knowledge and understanding are not for us finite mortals in this life. . . .

Every time I read the Bible God gives me a new Word, and I am grateful.

~

BIBLICAL WISDOM

I appeal to you therefore, brothers and sisters, by the mercies of God, to present your bodies as a living sacrifice, holy and acceptable to God, which is your spiritual worship. Romans 12:1

SILENCE FOR MEDITATION

QUESTIONS TO PONDER

- Do you ever belittle or berate yourself for a lack of understanding? According to Madeleine, our limits and failures are an important part of our humanness. How might you begin to overcome being too hard on yourself?
- Did you read the Bible today? If so, what "new Word" has God given you today? How will you share it with those around you? If not, why not?
- Someone has wisely said: "The only answer to life is more of life." In the context of what you have learned in this 40-day journey, what does that mean to you?

PSALM FRAGMENT

The fear of the LORD is the beginning of wisdom;
  all those who practice it have a good understanding.
His praise endures forever. Psalm 111:10

Journal Reflections

- What is "wisdom" to you? Write out a definition based on your study of Jesus' teachings.
- If your church follows a lectionary, begin the practice of reading the assigned passages before your worship service. Write down your personal thoughts about them in your journal.
- Madeleine in her many books has shared her own doubts and ambiguities about her faith, as well as her affirmations and certainties. Record some of your own doubts and ambiguities that still remain and make them a focus for your prayers in the weeks ahead.

Prayers of Hope & Healing

Pray for increased wisdom as you continue your journey with God and with the writings of saints ancient and modern in the days and weeks to come.

Prayer for Today

Lord God, show me how to become a living example of your work in Jesus Christ, that I may draw others to your worship and work. Amen.

Notes

Journey

Day 40
Sat 4/11

WORD

I, who live by words, am wordless when
I try my words in prayer. All language turns
To silence. Prayer will take my words and then
Reveal their emptiness. The stilled voice learns
To hold its peace, to listen with the heart
To silence that is joy, is adoration.
The self is shattered, all words torn apart
In this strange patterned time of contemplation
That, in time, breaks time, breaks words, breaks me.
And then, in silence, leaves me healed and mended.
I leave, returned to language, for I see
Through words, even when all words are ended.
I, who live by words, am wordless when
I turn me to the Word to pray. Amen.

BIBLICAL WISDOM

And the Word became flesh and lived among us, and we have seen his glory, the glory as of a father's only son, full of grace and truth. John 1:14

SILENCE FOR MEDITATION

QUESTIONS TO PONDER

- Words break down. Before God, only silence and adoration remain. When and how have you experienced this "end of words" in your life?
- Why is "the Word" the perfect metaphor for Jesus, his coming, his work, and his meaning for us?

- How have you experienced a changed attitude toward time, your human-ness, God's Word, prayer, exact answers, and the importance of other people through these weeks of your journey with Madeleine L'Engle? Be specific in your response.

PSALM FRAGMENT

For God alone my soul waits in silence;
from him comes my salvation. Psalm 62:1

JOURNAL REFLECTIONS

- Madeleine writes powerfully of how finally "all language turns to silence. . . . To silence that is joy, is adoration." Where, in your life, do you experience such silence?
- She writes of "this strange patterned time of contemplation / That, in time, breaks time, breaks words, breaks me. / And then, in silence, leaves me healed and mended." If you practice contemplative prayer, how does Madeleine's experience relate to yours? If you don't practice contemplative prayer, is there someone who might teach it to you or a book in which you could read about it?
- Go back and read through your journal entries and discover whether some of your earlier perceptions have been stretched by the discoveries you have made along the way. Write your conclusions in your journal.

PRAYERS OF HOPE & HEALING

Pray that we may all more deeply know Christ the Word among us in his transforming power, his eternal love, and his unending glory.

PRAYER FOR TODAY

Christ be with us, Christ above us, Christ beside us, Christ within us. Amen.

NOTES

Journey's End

You have finished your *40-Day Journey with Madeleine L'Engle*. I hope it has been a good journey and that along the way you have learned much, experienced much, and found good resources to deepen your faith and practice. As a result of this journey:

- How are you different?
- What have you learned?
- What have you experienced?
- In what ways have your faith and practice been transformed?

Notes

FOR FURTHER READING

And It Was Good. Wheaton, Ill.: Harold Shaw Publishers, 1983.

Awaiting the Child: An Advent Journal. Isabel Anders. Introduction by Madeleine L'Engle. Cambridge, Mass.: Cowley Publications, 1987, 2005.

A Circle of Quiet. HarperSanFrancisco, 1972.

A Cry Like a Bell. Wheaton, Ill.: Harold Shaw Publishers, 1987.

The Faces of Friendship. Isabel Anders, interview with Madeleine L'Engle, chapter 10. Eugene, Or.: Wipf & Stock Publishers, 2008.

Glimpses of Grace: Daily Thoughts and Reflections. With Carole F. Chase. HarperSanFrancisco, 1997.

The Irrational Season. San Francisco: Harper & Row, 1977.

Penguins and Golden Calves. Colorado Springs, Col.: Shaw Books, 1996, 2003.

A Stone for a Pillow. Wheaton, Ill.: Harold Shaw Publishers, 1986.

The Summer of the Great-Grandmother. HarperSanFrancisco, 1974.

Walking on Water. Wheaton, Ill.: Harold Shaw Publishers, 1980.

The Weather of the Heart. Wheaton, Ill.: Harold Shaw Publishers, 1978.

A Wrinkle in Time. New York: Dell Publishing, 1962.

The Young Unicorns. New York: Farrar, Straus and Giroux, 1968.

SOURCES

Day 1: *A Circle of Quiet*, pp. 158–159

Day 2: *Walking on Water*, pp. 18–19

Day 3: *Penguins and Golden Calves*, p. 41

Day 4: *The Irrational Season*, p. 171

Day 5: *A Wrinkle in Time*, p. 199

Day 6: *The Irrational Season*, p. 48

Day 7: *Walking on Water*, p. 55

Day 8: *Walking on Water*, p. 57

Day 9: *Penguins and Golden Calves*, p. 83

Day 10: New Year's Form letter, dated Feb. 1997

Day 11: *The Weather of the Heart*, p. 45

Day 12: *Walking on Water*, pp. 59–60

Day 13: *Christianity Today*, June 8, 1979

Day 14: *Christianity Today*, June 8, 1979

Day 15: *A Cry Like a Bell*, p. 23

Day 16: *A Circle of Quiet*, p. 11

Day 17: *The Weather of the Heart*, p. 49

Day 18: *Christianity Today*, June 8, 1979

Day 19: *The Young Unicorns*, pp. 144–145

Day 20: *A Stone for a Pillow*, p. 86

Day 21: *Walking on Water*, p. 62

We gratefully acknowledge the publishers who granted permission to reprint material from the following sources:

"After Annunciation," by Madeleine L'Engle. Copyright © 1996 by Crosswicks, Ltd. All rights reserved.

"Epiphany," by Madeleine L'Engle. Copyright © 1996 by Madeleine L'Engle and Luci Shaw.

A Circle of Quiet, by Madeleine L'Engle. Copyright © 1972 by Madeleine L'Engle Franklin. All rights reserved. Reprinted by permission of Farrar, Straus & Giroux.

The Irrational Season, by Madeleine L'Engle. Copyright © 1977 by Crosswicks, Ltd. All rights reserved. Reprinted by permission of HarperCollins, Publishers.

Penguins and Golden Calves: Icons and Idols, by Madeleine L'Engle. Copyright © 1996, 2003 by Crosswicks, Inc. Used by permission of WaterBrook Press, Colorado Springs, CO. All rights reserved.

"Pharaoh's Cross" from *A Cry Like a Bell*, by Madeleine L'Engle; Copyright © 1987 Crosswicks, Ltd

Walking on Water, by Madeleine L'Engle. Copyright © 1980, 1998, 2001 by Crosswicks, Inc. Used by permission of WaterBrook Press, Colorado Springs, CO. All rights reserved.

The Weather of the Heart, by Madeleine L'Engle. Copyright © 1978 Crosswicks, Ltd. Used by permission.

NOTES

NOTES